The Outdoor Toddler Activity Book

The Outdoor Toddler Activity Book

100+ Fun Early Learning Activities for Outside Play

Krissy Bonning-Gould

Illustrations by Natascha Rosenberg

ROCKRIDGE PRESS

For general information on our other products and services or to obtain technical support, please contact our Customer Care Department within the United States at (866) 744-2665, or outside the United States at (510) 253-0500.

Rockridge Press publishes its books in a variety of electronic and print formats. Some content that appears in print may not be available in electronic books, and vice versa.

Interior and Cover Designer: Suzanne LaGasa
Photo Art Director: Sue Bischofberger
Editor: Susan Randol
Production Editor: Andrew Yackira
Illustration © Natascha Rosenberg
Photography © Iryna Inshyna/Shutterstock, p. ii; © MNStudio/Shutterstock, p. xii; © jean schweitzer/Shutterstock, p. 14; © staticnak1983/iStock, p. 40; © sborisov/iStock, p. 68; © Melpomenem/iStock, p. 94; © kate_sept2004/iStock, p. 122; © Leo Rivas/ Unsplash, p. 148

ISBN: Print 978-1-64152-351-6 | eBook 978-1-64152-352-3

R1

*To my once-busy-toddlers, Sawyer, Priscilla, and
J.C., who are now speeding
through adolescence and tweenhood.*

*Slow down, please.
Mama's heart can't keep up.*

Contents

CHAPTER 3: **Run, Jump, and Play! 41**

CHAPTER 4: **Embrace Nature 69**

CHAPTER 5: **Get Wet!** 95

CHAPTER 6: **Outdoor Art 123**

- 1 -
OUTDOOR FUN

If there's one thing I learned from parenting three kids through their early years, it's that *toddlers are busy.* Sure, each of my three kids is unique and has, therefore, lovingly gifted me with their own unique parenting challenges throughout the past twelve years of mother-hood. But all three kids shared this in common between the ages of one and three: They were very curious, very energetic toddlers.

As you'll learn upon reading my personal toddler-parenting journey later in this chapter, I discovered a valuable tool for making the most of those sometimes-challenging toddler days: *PLAY!*

The activities shared throughout this book were designed to make it easier for you to add more intentional play, meaningful connection, learning opportunities, and *plain old fun* to your days with your own busy toddler.

My Toddler-Parenting Toolbox

Despite the child development courses I took in college and my experience managing art classes of feisty children wielding glue and scissors, I learned quickly that nothing adequately prepares a person to parent a toddler.

My son, Sawyer, was just nearing toddlerhood when I resigned from my art teaching position so our new little family could relocate for his dad's career. That summer, we transitioned from living right down the dirt road from my supportive parents and the old farmhouse where I grew up to living in a tiny apartment in an unfamiliar city. And I transitioned to a new role as a stay-at-home mom to a soon-to-be busy toddler, hundreds of miles away from any family and friends.

I quickly found myself missing the creativity and intellectual challenge of my teaching days. But creative activities with my toddler, Sawyer, (and soon with his sister, Priscilla, and little brother, J.C., too) were the only creativity a tired mama could muster. So, between diaper changes and nap-times, I added creative fun into our days and shared those ideas on my blog, B-InspiredMama.com, as a way to connect with other mothers and give my toddler-soaked brain some grown-up time.

Soon enough, creating and playing with my kids, which admittedly started in self-interest, turned into the most valuable tool in my toddler-parenting toolbox.

The Benefits of Outdoor Play

An American Academy of Pediatrics clinical report asserts the benefits of play as "extensive and well documented," helping children improve their "executive functioning, language, early math skills (numerosity and spatial concepts), social development, peer relations, [and] physical development and health." The report further details how outdoor play opportunities in particular, which often encourage children's active participation, aid in the development of motor skills, cognition, social skills, and language.

On top of all those excellent developmental benefits, we can't forget another benefit of taking play outside: Keeping toddler-size messes outside. I know how hard it can be to say "YES!" to potentially messy toddler activities when you just cleaned Cheerios off the living room floor. But exploring messy materials offers sensory experiences crucial for little growing bodies and complex sensory systems. Avoiding the mess can mean limiting the fun and learning. So the activities in this book aim to help you take the fun outside where you can embrace sometimes-messy active play and harness the benefits!

Toddler Time

Isn't it extraordinary how much learning and growth happen in the first few years of life? Toddlers have an inherently intense curiosity about the world around them. Their excitement over every new discovery and newly acquired skill is palpable and infectious. In my experience, watching a toddler learn and develop, moment by moment and day by day, is one of the most rewarding aspects of being a parent or caregiver.

A word of warning from a mom who's been there: Try not to let all those developmental milestones consume you. While your toddler's development is important to monitor with the guidance of your pediatrician, anxiety over precisely meeting milestones can impede your relationship and connection with your toddler. It may seem clichéd, but it's so true: Every child develops at their own pace and in their own way. So take the following milestones into consideration when choosing developmentally appropriate activities for your child, but always follow your gut instincts and your little one's lead regarding what is *just right* for them.

Now, let's take a quick look at all the incredible learning and development happening in our toddlers, ages one through three years.

12 to 18 Months

Rapid physical growth throughout infancy starts to slow as babies reach their first birthday and move into toddlerhood. The focus shifts, instead, to how their bodies interact in space and the world around them while they work on mastering new skills. Here are some specific skills that start emerging:

Gross Motor Skills:

- Stands without support
- Walks with few falls
- Squats to pick something up
- Sits independently on a chair
- Climbs stairs or furniture
- Tosses a ball underhand while seated

Fine Motor Skills:

- Claps hands
- Waves goodbye
- Holds a crayon and scribbles
- Uses fingertips to pick up small objects
- Drinks from a cup
- Uses a spoon
- Scoops materials for play
- Stacks a couple objects
- Bangs objects together

Language and Social-Emotional Development:

- Continues babbling
- May use 5 to 10 words
- Points at familiar people and objects in pictures
- Imitates others during play
- Can identify a couple body parts
- Shakes head to respond to yes/no questions
- Follows simple directions
- Has an interest in interacting with people
- Can locate objects pointed to
- Turns head in response to hearing own name

18 to 24 Months

As toddlers approach their second birthday, social and play skills expand. While they still primarily imitate during play, they start to interact more with others and even delve into some pretend play. Here are some specific skills they often exhibit:

Gross Motor Skills:

- Walks and runs
- Coordinates movements for play
- Jumps with feet together
- Walks up and down stairs
- Throws a ball into a box
- Uses ride-on toys

Fine Motor Skills:

- Uses fingers and thumb to hold a crayon
- Opens containers
- Turns the pages of a book
- Scribble-writes with writing tools
- Builds with 4 or more blocks
- Turns over and pours out containers

Language and Social-Emotional Skills:

- Starts to use 2-word phrases
- Can name objects in pictures
- Understands action words
- Starts to use pronouns (you, my, me)
- Can identify 3 to 5 body parts
- Follows simple 2-step directions
- Turns head when hearing own name
- Interacts with others during play
- May play with toys without mouthing them
- Enjoys directing play

24 to 36 Months

After toddlers turn two years old, their cognitive, language, and social-emotional learning take center stage over the previous year's focus on physical development. That social-emotional growth brings along toddlers' desire for more independence, though. That—combined with expanding language skills helping them communicate their wants (and their "NO!"s)—can prove to be quite challenging. Here are the important skills they're developing:

Gross Motor Skills:

- Kicks a ball forward
- Can stand on tiptoes
- Pulls toys behind while walking
- Carries large toys while walking
- Can ride a tricycle
- Catches a large ball
- Jumps over an object
- Walks along a balance beam

Fine Motor Skills:

- Uses a pincer grasp to pick up small objects
- Turns door handles
- Screws lid on a container
- Can string large beads
- Starts to draw squares and circles

Language and Social-Emotional Skills:

- Uses 2- to 4-word sentences
- Talks understandably
- Demonstrates increasing independence
- Plays make-believe
- Begins to sort objects by colors and shapes
- Starts to understand "same" and "different"
- Enjoys listening to and telling stories
- Starts to count and understand numbers
- Becomes increasingly inventive during play

Each outdoor toddler activity in this book has been labeled with helpful icons indicating the developmental skills or learning concepts it strengthens, making it easy to choose developmentally appropriate activities for your toddler.

However, I designed each of the activities with the already inherent benefits of play in mind, harnessing the most beneficial parts—*curiosity, creativity, sensory experiences, social-emotional learning*, and *problem-solving*—to inspire authentic learning, creativity, and connection. Those already present, powerful qualities of your toddler's play naturally advance development and strengthen skills!

So definitely reference the developmental milestones and skills icons when choosing appropriate activities for your child. And consider the activities' suggestions for enhancing specific skills and inspiring learning, but *always, always, always follow your child's natural curiosity and creativity above all else.*

Skills Learned

 colors

 listening

problem-solving

 creativity

 memory

 science

 early literacy

mindfulness

sensory development

 fine motor skills

123 numbers and counting

shapes and letters

 gross motor skills

 oral motor development

 social-emotional development

 imagination

 patterns

 sorting

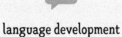 language development

 visual spatial skills

Safety First!

You'll notice some activities include a note of **Caution!** While designing the activities, I tried to put my toddler-cap on to imagine possible safety concerns. Use these notes of caution to determine which activities are a good fit for your child and situation, and implement them for optimal safety. But ultimately, follow these general safety guidelines during any activity with your toddler:

- Consider your toddler's development and abilities when choosing activities. Monitor and assist, as needed, when trying advanced activities.

- Avoid activities with small materials if your toddler mouths objects during play.

- *Always* supervise closely during water play, and never leave bins, buckets, or pools of water unattended.

- Keep your toddler away from sharp scissors, knives, hot glue guns, and other potentially hazardous tools. If possible, do any prep requiring these tools when your toddler is napping or not present.

- Whenever possible, choose nontoxic, kid-friendly art supplies and materials. If a material is new to you and likely to come in contact with your toddler's skin, test it on a small area before play.

- Always use sunscreen during outdoor play, and remember to reapply after water play and according to the package instructions.

- Always check your child for rashes, skin irritations, and ticks after outdoor play, especially when playing in tall grasses or new areas.

- Check the temperature of outdoor play surfaces, like slides and swings, before use on warm days.

- Some play materials and setups could pose tripping, slipping, falling, choking, and strangulation hazards if left unsupervised. Take down and put away all play setups after play has ended.

- All of the activities are designed for your toddler *and you*. Always supervise during play.

How to Use This Book

As mentioned earlier, my hope for this book of over 100 outdoor toddler activities is to make it *easier* for you to incorporate more intentional play, meaningful connection, playful learning, and fun into your days with your toddler. Here are some tips to maximize the joy:

Get outside, get active, and get messy! The activities have been sorted into five toddler-friendly types (each type in its own chapter): messy play, active games and play, nature-based activities, water activities, and outdoor arts and crafts. All of these are particularly suited to an outdoor environment, where toddlers can get messy, explore nature, run around, and make lots of noise.

Don't let the weather hinder the fun. Outdoor play doesn't have to be limited to warm sunny days. I've tried to sprinkle in activities suited to different weather conditions and seasons. Plus, each chapter includes a sidebar highlighting an activity perfect for a particular season or family vacation spot.

Keep it simple. I know firsthand how play and learning activities need to be easy to implement or they may *never* happen. That's why I've made sure the activities use materials found around the house. Most activities require five materials or less. Many use basic kids' craft supplies, like tape, washable paint, or pom-poms. Some use typical toddler toys, like toy trucks, letter magnets, or sidewalk chalk. Other activities utilize everyday household objects, such as plastic storage bins, zip-top bags, bottles and boxes from the recycling bin, or aluminum foil. A few of the activities require *no materials at all!* Plus, all activities were designed to require little to no prep, and any prep required is made easy with clear steps and a time estimate. Keep things simple by using what you have around the house and prepping ahead of time when needed.

Consider your toddler's attention span. I've tailored each activity to a toddler-size attention span, keeping play active and no more than 20 minutes from start to finish. The activities include time estimates for prep (if there is any) and the activity itself. Choose the ones that match your toddler's attention span, and don't force your toddler to complete activities after he loses interest.

Follow your toddler's lead. While each of the activities focuses on one or more developmental skill, that learning should never be forced in a way that inhibits the natural joy of play and connection between you and your little one. With toddlers' inclination for independence, they will surely let you know when they don't want to do something! *Always follow your toddler's lead.*

Don't try to do it all. I wouldn't expect you to read this entire book in one sitting or follow the activities in order. Who has time for that with a toddler running around?! Instead, grab it at the beginning of the week to plan one activity for each day. Take a quick peek to find some inspiration before you head outside or mark your favorite activities to come back to when you need a positive reset in your day with your toddler.

Remember that every little bit of play and connection counts! Don't feel pressured to do every activity in this book. You can't do it all. But, with my busy toddlers, Sawyer, Priscilla, and J.C., racing through childhood and even *(groan . . .)* tweenhood now, I'm seeing firsthand how every little bit of creativity, intentional play, and connection in those early years can have positive returns far beyond them.

Ultimately, remember to keep the stress and pressure low and the creativity, connection, and fun high!

- 2 -
MAKE IT MESSY!

I know what you're thinking: You're already dealing with enough messes from ice cream accidents to potty training mishaps to toddler spaghetti splatters. Cleaning up another mess is *not* on your to-do list.

Whether we like the mess or not, toddlers benefit immensely from messy play. Experiencing diverse textures and materials aids in the development and regulation of their complex sensory system. Plus, some of the best messy materials offer opportunities for practicing motor skills, problem-solving strategies, and creativity.

So put the kids in their play clothes or swimsuits, grab some old towels, and have the hose on standby because we're going outside for some messy fun!

Mud-Print Patterns

Do your toddler's hands and feet gravitate toward mud? You might as well embrace it with this muddy learning opportunity.

Messiness: 5
Prep Time: None
Activity Time: 10 minutes

MATERIALS:

Mud

STEPS

1. Have your toddler find a large patch of squishy mud.

2. Invite him to squish a handprint into the mud. Have him squish a footprint into the mud next to the handprint.

3. Repeat, making a simple AB pattern (handprint, footprint, handprint, footprint . . .).

4. Extend the learning by trying more complex patterns, such as an AAB pattern (handprint, handprint, footprint, handprint, handprint, footprint . . .). Have your toddler smooth the mud with his hand between patterns.

TIP *No mud? No problem! Spray a large patch of dirt with the hose to make some.*

Sprinkles & Cream Mud-Pie Bakery

Make this childhood classic even more memorable with old kitchen items and a couple of special ingredients.

Messiness: 5
Prep Time: None
Activity Time: 30 minutes

MATERIALS

Mud and dirt

Water

Mixing bowls, measuring cups, and utensils

Pie pans, metal or aluminum foil

Shaving cream

Sequins or small beads

STEPS

1. Invite your toddler to use the various kitchen items to mix, stir, pour, bake, and serve mud pies.

2. Encourage the use of shaving cream and sequins as pretend whipped cream and sprinkles.

TIP *Find inexpensive mixing bowls, utensils, and pie pans at thrift stores or yard sales. Store them in a plastic dish drainer or bin for a dedicated mud-pie-making kit.*

CAUTION! *Make sure your toddler understands that none of the mud-pie ingredients and creations are actually edible. This activity may not be suitable for children who put objects in their mouths during play.*

SKILLS
LEARNED

sensory
development

fine
motor skills

numbers
and counting

123

Digging for Worms

Does your toddler still put things in her mouth during play or make giant messes during sensory play? Taking this taste-safe sensory activity outside is a great solution.

Messiness: 5
Prep Time: None
Activity Time: 15 minutes

MATERIALS

5 to 10 gummy candy worms

Cake pan and spatula

4 cups chocolate pudding

5 chocolate sandwich cookies

Sandwich-size plastic zip-top bag

Kids' tweezers (optional)

STEPS

1. Have your toddler count out and add the candy worms to the cake pan, and spread the pudding evenly over the worms.

2. Help crush the sandwich cookies inside a sealed zip-top bag, then sprinkle them evenly over the wormy pudding mixture.

3. Invite your toddler to dig into the mixture with her fingers to find the worms. Offer some plastic kids' tweezers for grabbing worms, too, if you have them.

4. Encourage her to count the worms as she finds them.

CAUTION! *Monitor your child closely as the materials used can be a choking hazard. This activity may not be suitable for toddlers who cannot chew sufficiently.*

Squishy Sensory Walk

Sensory walks are incredibly versatile. Use different materials in the bins each time you do this activity to give your toddler's toes an entirely new sensory experience.

Messiness: 4
Prep Time: 5 minutes
Activity Time: 10 minutes

MATERIALS

Medium shallow plastic bins, one per textured material

Materials of various textures, such as cooked pasta, cotton balls, bubble wrap, washable paint, ice cubes, and shaving cream

PREP

Line the bins up in a row and add a different textured material to each one.

STEPS

1. Have your toddler walk through the row of bins, stepping into one bin after another.

2. Ask him to describe what his feet feel in each bin. Encourage descriptive words like *soft, bumpy, hard, squishy, slimy,* and *wet.*

Sparkly Snow Volcano

Skip the same old snowman on a winter day and try this frosty version of a classic science experiment instead.

Messiness: 4
Prep Time: None
Activity Time: 20 minutes

MATERIALS

Tall plastic cup

Snow

2 tablespoons baking soda

1 tablespoon glitter

1 ½ cups vinegar

Food coloring

Large measuring cup and spoon

STEPS

1. Place the cup into the snow on the ground, and have your toddler help build the snow into a volcano shape around the cup. Keep the cup free of snow and leave an opening at the top.

2. Add the baking soda and glitter to the cup through the opening in the top of the volcano.

3. Pour the vinegar into a large measuring cup, and have your toddler help color the vinegar with a few drops of food coloring.

4. Help your little one pour the vinegar into the snow volcano and enjoy the sparkly eruption!

Swirly Soap Foamy Ocean

Let's get those bath toys out of the bathtub and into their very own outdoor foamy ocean.

Messiness: 4
Prep Time: 10 minutes
Activity Time: 20 minutes

MATERIALS

Water

Mixing bowl

Liquid soap

Washable paint, in blue and green

Immersion hand blender or electric hand mixer

Large shallow plastic bin

Water-friendly toys

PREP

1. Pour a couple inches of water into the mixing bowl, then add a generous squirt each of soap and blue paint. Use the hand blender to blend the mixture until you have blue soap foam. Blend in more soap, paint, or water as needed for desired color and foamy consistency. Add the soap foam to one side of the bin.

2. Repeat, using the green paint to make green soap foam, and add it to the bin beside the blue foam.

STEPS

1. Invite your child to gently swirl the two colors of foam together with her fingers to create a pretty marbled effect.

2. Have her take her toys for a swim in the swirly foam ocean.

3. Encourage imaginative play, especially silly soap foam hairdos on any doll or animal toys!

CAUTION! *Always supervise your toddler closely around water.*

SKILLS
LEARNED

visual
spatial skills

gross
motor skills

colors

Stomp & Splash Sidewalk Rainbow

The splashing colors make this outdoor activity educational, while the stomping helps use up some of that endless toddler energy!

Messiness: 5
Prep Time: 10 minutes
Activity Time: 15 minutes

MATERIALS

Washable paint, in red, orange, yellow, green, blue, and purple

Water

6 sandwich-size plastic zip-top bags

Straw

Medium plastic bin

PREP

1. Add a generous squirt of paint and a cup or so of water to a zip-top bag. Place a straw into the bag and seal the bag around the straw.

2. Hold the bag and straw, and gently blow air into the bag through the straw.

3. Pull out the straw as you seal the zip-top bag, capturing the air inside. Shake the bag gently to mix the paint and carefully set it aside in a plastic bin.

4. Repeat with each color of paint in its own zip-top bag.

STEPS

1. Place the paint-filled bags on the sidewalk in the order of the rainbow: red, orange, yellow, green, blue, and purple.

2. Have your toddler STOMP the bags, in rainbow order, popping them and splashing the paint to make a messy but beautiful sidewalk rainbow. Encourage him to shout each color as he stomps.

3. Alternatively, place the bags randomly along the sidewalk, then call out colors for your toddler to find and STOMP!

TIP *If you're concerned about the paint staining the sidewalk, do the activity on white roll paper or a large sheet of cardboard.*

CAUTION! *Make sure your toddler uses only one foot to stomp. Jumping on a bag with both feet could result in slipping and injury.*

Soapy Stripes

This easy soap-based recipe results in silky-smooth, kid-friendly body paint, perfect for some creative fun in the kiddie pool.

Messiness: 5
Prep Time: 10 minutes
Activity Time: 20 minutes

MATERIALS

1 cup kid-friendly liquid soap

¼ to ½ cup cornstarch

Mixing bowl and spatula

6-cup muffin pan

Washable paint

Paintbrushes

CAUTION! *Using kid-friendly soap and nontoxic washable paint should result in a nonirritating, nonstaining body paint. However, test your homemade mixture on a small area of skin before painting. Always supervise your toddler closely around water.*

PREP

1. Add the soap and ¼ cup of cornstarch to a mixing bowl, and stir until thoroughly combined. Mix in additional cornstarch, as needed, for the desired paint-like consistency.

2. Divide the mixture evenly between the muffin pan cups. Mix a different color of paint into the soap mixture in each muffin pan cup.

3. Get your swimsuits on and take your pan of soap body paint to the kiddie pool.

STEPS

1. In or near the kiddie pool, paint colorful stripes with the homemade body paint on your toddler's arms and legs. Invite your child to paint stripes on your arms and legs, too.

2. Explore simple patterns by alternating the colors of the stripes.

3. Wash the soapy stripes off in the kiddie pool, then paint some more!

TIP *Painting stripes allows you to explore patterns, but you could also paint letters, numbers, shapes, or just silly polka dots.*

sensory
development

fine
motor skills

SKILLS
LEARNED

Slimy Insect Fun

Slime-making has currently captivated my ten-year-old—but it can be toddler-friendly, too. Just use taste-safe ingredients and take the messy slime-fest outside!

Messiness: **4**
Prep Time: **None**
Activity Time: **20 minutes**

MATERIALS

1 (0.6-ounce) box sugar-free green gelatin

1 cup cornstarch

Mixing bowl and spoon

Water

Small plastic insect toys

STEPS

1. Help your toddler add the dry ingredients to the mixing bowl and stir to combine.

2. Add a couple tablespoons of water and stir thoroughly. Repeat, adding a couple tablespoons of water at a time, until the mixture pulls from the sides of the bowl and forms a slime.

3. Let your toddler knead and explore the slime mixture. Add more water or cornstarch, as needed, to adjust the slime's consistency.

4. Give your toddler some small insect toys for exploring with the slime.

CAUTION! *While this slime is taste-safe, it isn't fully edible. This activity may not be suitable for children who put objects in their mouths during play.*

Take a Coffee Break

Getting bored with the same old pretend tea party play? Make some homemade coffee-scented playdough with your toddler for a visit to the coffee shop instead! Taking the messy playdough-making outside makes it stress-free and fun.

Messiness: **4**
Prep Time: **None**
Activity Time: **20 minutes**

MATERIALS

Playdough
(recipe on page 27, or store-bought)

½ cup dry
coffee grounds

Cooking oil (optional)

Warm water (optional)

Plastic dishes, cups, and utensils

Sugar

STEPS

1. Invite your toddler to help knead the coffee grounds into the playdough. Add small amounts of oil or water at a time, as needed, until it reaches the desired consistency.

2. Encourage her to use her homemade coffee play-dough to play pretend coffee shop.

3. Inspire counting practice by requesting your coffee with a certain number of spoonfuls of sugar or requesting a specific number of playdough cookies on the side.

4. Model manners and social skills for your toddler, such as using please and thank you, making polite conversation, and showing kindness.

CAUTION! *Although the homemade playdough is taste-safe, it is not fully edible.*

Basic Playdough

MATERIALS

2 cups flour

½ cup salt

2 tablespoons cream of tartar

Mixing bowls and spoon

1 to 2 tablespoons any cooking oil

1 to 2 cups warm water

Make homemade playdough with your toddler by adding the dry ingredients to a mixing bowl, and stir them to combine.

Add the wet ingredients to a separate bowl, and stir to combine.

Slowly add the wet ingredient mixture to the dry ingredients, stirring to combine until a dough starts to form and pull from the sides of the bowl.

Have your toddler knead the dough until it reaches a soft, nonsticky playdough consistency. Knead in more flour or water, as needed.

SKILLS
LEARNED | fine
motor skills | visual
spatial skills | numbers
and counting | imagination

123

Spaghetti & Meatballs Scoop & Count

Cooked spaghetti is a great taste-safe sensory material for little ones. The addition of pretend meatballs allows for some fine motor work and counting practice, too. The cooked spaghetti can get sticky and unwieldy for toddlers just learning to scoop, so take this one outdoors where the mess won't matter.

Messiness: 3
Prep Time: 10 minutes + cooling time
Activity Time: 15 minutes

MATERIALS

1 (16-ounce) package spaghetti, cooked according to package

Medium plastic bin

Red construction paper

Spaghetti serving spoon and plastic dishware

Vegetable oil (optional)

STEPS

1. Add the cooked spaghetti to a plastic bin.

2. Invite your toddler to help make "meatballs" for the spaghetti by crumpling red construction paper into round balls. Help him practice counting as he puts the meatballs in the bin.

3. Allow him some free play time exploring the spaghetti and meatballs in the bin with a serving spoon and various plastic dishware. Encourage imaginative play.

4. Challenge your toddler by asking him to serve you a plate of spaghetti with a certain number of meatballs.

TIP *Stir a tablespoon or two of vegetable oil into the cooked spaghetti before play to keep it from sticking together.*

CAUTION! *Keep your toddler away from the stove and hot ingredients. This activity may not be suitable for children who put objects in their mouths during play.*

Toy Truck Tracks

Keep the outdoor doughy fun going by using your leftover playdough for some messy truck-themed shape learning.

Messiness: **4**
Prep Time: **None**
Activity Time: **15 minutes**

MATERIALS

Playdough
(recipe on page 27,
or store-bought)

Rolling pin (optional)

Small stick (optional)

Toy truck

STEPS

1. Help your toddler flatten out the playdough using a rolling pin or your hands. Use a small stick or a finger to draw a large basic shape in the flattened playdough.

2. Have your child drive a toy truck along the lines of the shape, making tire tracks in the playdough.

3. Flatten the playdough, and repeat with each basic shape: circle, square, triangle, rectangle, diamond, and oval.

TIP *Knead a little bit of warm water or oil into your leftover dough if it needs softening.*

CAUTION! *Although the homemade playdough is taste-safe, it is not fully edible.*

Painted Picnic Tablecloth

Grab an inexpensive white fabric tablecloth from your local thrift store or dollar store, and let the kids have some messy fun squirt-painting it. If you use acrylic paint, you can use your new colorful tablecloth for future family picnics.

Messiness: 5
Prep Time: 5 minutes
Activity Time: 20 minutes

MATERIALS

Squeeze bottles

Acrylic paint

Water

White fabric tablecloth

PREP

1. Fill each squeeze bottle about three-quarters of the way with paint, using a different color for each bottle. Add water to each bottle, if necessary, to thin it for squirting.

2. Lay the tablecloth out on a dry outdoor surface or hang it over a fence.

STEPS

1. Have your toddler use the paint-filled squeeze bottles to squirt paint on the tablecloth.

2. Encourage her to squirt the paint any way she wants.

3. Want to keep this colorful tablecloth? Allow it to dry fully in the sunshine, then put it in the dryer on high heat for 30 minutes to set the paint.

TIP *Find squeeze bottles right in your recycling bin. Simply use empty clean ketchup, salad dressing, and other condiment bottles.*

Sparkly Milk Fireworks

This toddler-friendly science experiment is perfect for celebrating the Fourth of July. Change up the colors, and you can pair it with any holiday or celebration.

Messiness: 2
Prep Time: None
Activity Time: 10 minutes

MATERIALS

Pie pan

Full-fat milk

Food coloring, red and blue

Glitter

Cotton swab

Small bowl of dish soap

STEPS

1. Fill the bottom of the pie pan with milk. Have your toddler help add some drops of food coloring and shakes of glitter.

2. Have him dip a cotton swab in the dish soap, then touch the swab to the surface of the milk.

3. Watch the excitement as he sees the fireworks of color and glitter swirl and dart away from the soapy cotton swab.

SEASONAL ACTIVITY

SKILLS
LEARNED
sensory
development

visual
spatial skills

science

Sandbox Streams & Dams

Clean out your food storage container stash and put all those stray plastic lids to good use with some engineering play in the sandbox.

Messiness: 5
Prep Time: None
Activity Time: 20 minutes

MATERIALS

Up to 5 plastic food storage container lids, of various sizes

Sand in a sandbox

Cup and pail of water

Hose for water (optional)

STEPS

1. Help your child use plastic lids as tools for digging streambeds in the sandbox. Hold each side of a lid, then drag it along the sand to carve out streams. Encourage her to experiment with other ways she can use the lids as tools, such as for scooping sand or pressing marks into it.

2. Use the cup to add small amounts of water, as needed, to pack the bottom and sides of the streambeds so they hold their form.

3. Help your child fill her streams with water using the cup and pail or a hose.

4. Help her experiment with damming the water with the plastic lids by pushing them into the sand across her streams.

CAUTION! *Always supervise your toddler closely around water.*

Foam-Fun ABCs

This one-ingredient activity makes toddler writing practice super-easy. The mess factor makes it full of sensory excitement!

Messiness: **4**
Prep Time: **None**
Activity Time: **15 minutes**

MATERIALS

Shaving cream

Window

STEPS

1. Help your toddler squirt and smooth shaving cream onto an outside window.

2. With your finger, write the letter "A" in the shaving cream on the window. Have your toddler trace over it with her finger or have her write her own "A" next to yours.

3. Smooth the shaving cream, and repeat with each letter in the alphabet.

4. Use the hose to easily wash it all off the window when you're done.

CAUTION! *Shaving cream is a pretty common sensory play material, but if you haven't used it with your toddler before, test some on a small area of her skin before play. If it irritates her skin or she is apt to put her hands in her mouth during play, try using whipped cream instead.*

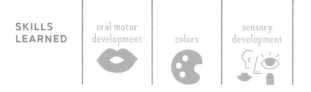
Milk Bubble Rainbow

What kid hasn't made a milk bubble mess on the kitchen table? Embrace your toddler's bubble-blowing inclinations by making a messy milk bubble rainbow outside. Blowing through the straw helps strengthen oral motor skills and regulate the sensory system.

Messiness: 3
Prep Time: None
Activity Time: 15 minutes

MATERIALS

6 small plastic food storage containers, clear

6 cups milk

Food coloring, in red, orange, yellow, green, blue, and purple

Spoon

Straw

STEPS

1. Have your toddler line the containers up in a row, and add about a cup of milk to each.

2. Use a few drops of food coloring in each container to turn the milk in each a different color of the rainbow. Let your toddler stir the milk in each container and watch it magically change color.

3. Have him use a straw to blow air into the red milk until red bubbles overflow the container. Repeat, with each container of colored milk to make a colorful overflowing milk bubble rainbow.

Number Excavation

Incorporate the mystery and excitement of excavation into your toddler's sand-box play!

Messiness: 5
Prep Time: 5 minutes
Activity Time: 20 minutes

MATERIALS

Foam bath number toys

Sand in a sandbox

Paintbrushes

PREP

Bury foam numbers in the sandbox, ideally without your toddler seeing you do so.

STEPS

1. Invite your child to an archaeology excavation in her sandbox, saying something like, "During archaeology excavations, scientists dig in the ground for things left behind by people and animals a long time ago."

2. Give her various paintbrushes and show her how to use them to brush the sand away from foam numbers as she finds them.

3. As she finds the numbers, help her identify each one and put them in order.

TIP *No foam bath numbers? No problem! Bury and dig for any small toys or natural objects.*

Slip, Slide & Mix Colors

Add some messy color-mixing excitement to the classic backyard waterslide!

Messiness: 5
Prep Time: 15 minutes
Activity Time: 20 minutes

MATERIALS

Large light gray
or white poly tarp,
or store-bought
backyard waterslide

Tent stakes

Brightly colored
plastic cups

Hose and sprinkler
with water

2 squeeze bottles

Kids' shampoo

Washable paint, in two
of the primary colors:
red, yellow, or blue

Funnel (optional)

PREP

1. Spread the tarp out on a slightly inclined section of lawn.

2. Use tent stakes to secure two corners of the tarp to the group, at the top of the incline. Cover any stake that sticks up from the ground with an upside-down, brightly colored plastic cup for safety.

3. Position the sprinkler near the top of the tarp so it sprays the entire thing.

4. Fill a squeeze bottle about one-third of the way with shampoo, and fill the rest of the way with paint. Shake to distribute the color. Repeat with the other squeeze bottle and color of paint.

5. Squirt one color of your homemade soap-paint generously on one side of the tarp, then the other color of soap-paint on the opposite side.

Have your toddler slide through one color, on one side of the tarp. Have her slide through the other color on the other side. Share in her excitement when she discovers how the paint mixed together on her body and the slide to make a new color. Repeat for more slippery color-mixing fun!

CAUTION! *Make sure the ground under and around the tarp is free of rocks, tree roots, sticks, or other hard, sharp objects. Supervise your toddler during play, and never leave the activity set up when not supervising, as the materials used can be a strangulation or injury hazard.*

SKILLS
LEARNED

gross
motor skills

visual
spatial skills

sorting

Kiddie Pool Gold Panning

Turn your toddler's kiddie pool into a gold panning adventure. Finding the treasure is exciting, plus the scooping and sifting provide excellent strengthening of gross motor skills.

Messiness: 4
Prep Time: 5 minutes
Activity Time: 20 minutes

MATERIALS

Gravel or sand

Kiddie pool

Toy gold coins
and gems

Hose with water

Metal pie pan

2 medium plastic food
storage containers

PREP

1. Add some gravel to the bottom of the kiddie pool.

2. Mix in some gold coins and gems.

3. Add water to a few inches above the gravel.

STEPS

1. Invite your toddler to use the pie pan to scoop up gravel and water, then shake it back and forth to pan for gold and gems.

2. Have him sort the gold coins and gems into different containers.

TIP *You could also do this activity in a large shallow plastic bin instead of a kiddie pool.*

CAUTION! *Always supervise your toddler closely around water. This activity may not be suitable for children who put objects in their mouths during play.*

Jiggly Gelatin Shapes

The use of gelatin makes this messy sensory activity perfect for young toddlers who still explore objects with their mouths. The addition of containers, scoops, and spoons inspires learning about shapes, size, and space.

Messiness: 4
Prep Time: 10 minutes
Activity Time: 20 minutes

MATERIALS

4 to 6 plastic food storage containers, various shapes and sizes

Baking sheet pan

Nonstick cooking spray

3 (0.6-ounce) boxes of different-flavored gelatin

Water

Stove and saucepan

Spoons and scoops

PREP

1. Place the containers on the sheet pan. Lightly spray the inside of each with cooking spray.

2. Prepare the gelatin according to package directions and pour it into the containers. Transfer the pan of containers into the refrigerator and refrigerate until set.

STEPS

1. With your toddler, flip each container over to unmold the gelatin shapes. Encourage him to identify each shape.

2. Mix up the containers and have him try to match each container to its corresponding gelatin shape.

3. Allow him time to explore the gelatin with the spoons, scoops, and containers.

CAUTION! *Keep your toddler away from the stove and hot ingredients. Monitor your child closely as the materials used can be a choking hazard. If possible, keep one small container of gelatin aside and cut it into bite-size pieces for safe snacking during play.*

- 3 -
RUN, JUMP, AND PLAY!

Remember me telling you back in chapter 1 just how *busy* my kids were as toddlers? My mom and I still joke about the nickname we assigned to my son, Sawyer: "the runner!" His little legs were always moving. With so much learning and development occurring in such a short period of time, who can blame toddlers for wanting to explore every nook and cranny of their world (and every breakable object in every store)?

The outdoor activities in this chapter are developed to get your toddler strengthening and coordinating gross motor skills, and hopefully burning some of that active energy, in an easy, educational, and fun way!

Giant Tic-Tac-Toss

Make simple sock beanbags for a giant active version of tic-tac-toe. Bonus: You can use the homemade beanbags for more active play as your toddler grows.

Messiness: 2
Prep Time: 10 minutes
Activity Time: 15 minutes

MATERIALS

10 old kids' socks,
5 each of two different
colors

3 to 6 (16-ounce) bags
dried beans

Rubber bands

Sidewalk chalk

Permanent marker
(optional)

PREP

1. Make 10 sock beanbags (5 of each color) by filling each sock with up to 1 cup of dried beans and closing it with a rubber band. Fold the loose sock end on each beanbag inside out, down over the bean-filled part.

2. Use sidewalk chalk to draw a giant three-by-three "#" tic-tac-toe board on the sidewalk or pavement.

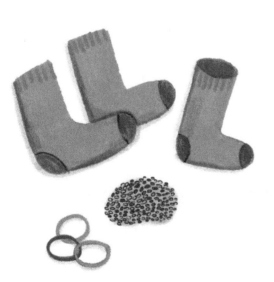

1. Have your toddler choose one color of beanbags, while you take the other color.

2. Take turns tossing your beanbags onto the giant tic-tac-toss board, following the rules of tic-tac-toe. If a beanbag lands in a space that already has one, just grab it and retoss.

3. The first person to get their beanbags in three spaces in a row wins.

TIP *If you only have white socks, use a permanent marker to draw a large "O" on 5 socks and a large "X" on the remaining 5 socks.*

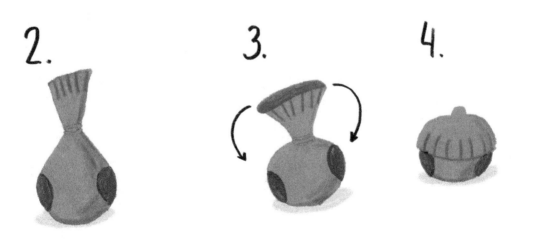

SKILLS
LEARNED

gross
motor skills

visual
spatial skills

colors

memory

Hanging Color Swat

Toddlers learning colors—or with lots of energy to expend—will love this balloon swatting game. And being outside, your child can swing away without any worry over breaking anything.

Messiness: 1
Prep Time: 10 minutes
Activity Time: 15 minutes

MATERIALS

Balloons in red, orange, yellow, green, blue, and purple

String

Scissors

Branch on a tree or outdoor playset bar

Flyswatter

PREP

1. Blow up and tie each balloon.

2. Use string to hang each balloon from a tree branch or high bar, making sure your toddler can reach the balloons with a flyswatter.

STEPS

1. Call out a color for your toddler to find and swat with the flyswatter.

2. Encourage him to shout out each color as he swats them.

3. For further listening and memory challenge, call out a sequence of three or more colors for your toddler to swat in order.

CAUTION! *Keep your toddler away from sharp objects. Monitor your child closely as the materials used can be a choking hazard. Supervise your toddler during play, and never leave the activity set up when not supervising, as the materials used can be a strangulation or injury hazard.*

Bowling on Wheels

Grab your toddler's ride-on toys for a bowling activity sure to get your child giggling!

Messiness: 2
Prep Time: 5 minutes
Activity Time: 15 minutes

MATERIALS

6 (2-liter) soda bottles

Water

Funnel (optional)

Food coloring (optional)

Permanent markers

Ride-on toys

PREP

1. Fill each bottle halfway with water. Use a funnel, if needed. Color the water in each bottle with a different color of food coloring, if desired.

2. Use a permanent marker to write a large number (1 through 6) on the side of each bottle.

STEPS

1. Position the numbered bottles in a row with a couple feet between each one, in numerical order.

2. With your toddler positioned on a ride-on toy a good distance away, call out one of the numbers for her to bowl down by riding toward and hitting it.

3. Have her return, then repeat, calling out the other numbers until she has bowled all the number pins down.

TIP *Not into number learning? Write letters of your child's name or the different basic shapes on the bottles instead.*

CAUTION! *Supervise your toddler during play, and never leave the activity set up when not supervising, as the materials used can be a strangulation or injury hazard.*

Bang & Clang Sound Station

There's no need for power tools to make this outdoor sound station; simply rescue some old kitchen items, tie them to the fence, and enjoy the joy-filled sounds of play and learning!

Messiness: 2
Prep Time: 20 minutes
Activity Time: 20 minutes

MATERIALS

Metal and plastic kitchen items, such as pots, pans, containers, lids, and colanders

Cable ties and/or cord

Heavy-duty scissors or utility knife

Fence or deck railing

Pail with handle

Wooden spoons

PREP

1. Gather old kitchen items or find affordable ones at a thrift store or yard sale. Ideally, choose items that already have holes or handles for easier hanging.

2. Use cable ties and/or cord to mount the kitchen items onto the fence. Trim loose ends.

3. Add a hanging pail to hold the wooden spoons.

STEPS

1. Invite your toddler to explore sound by using the wooden spoons to bang and clang on the items on her new sound station.

2. Have her try making beats and even sing along.

TIP *Live in an apartment? Make your sound station on a wooden pallet, which can be moved or stored away.*

CAUTION! *Keep your toddler away from sharp objects. Supervise your toddler during play, and never leave the activity set up when not supervising, as the materials used can be a strangulation or injury hazard.*

SKILLS
LEARNED | gross
motor skills | fine
motor skills | visual
spatial skills

Laundry Line Relay

This activity is a win-win: Your toddler gets playful motor skills practice, while you get your toddler learning helpful laundry skills!

Messiness: 1
Prep Time: 5 minutes
Activity Time: 15 minutes

MATERIALS

Rope

2 trees, swing-set poles, or lawn chairs

Laundry basket filled with socks, washcloths, or dishcloths

Clothespins

Timer (optional)

PREP

Tie a rope between two objects, such as poles or trees that are around 5 to 10 feet apart, to make a temporary toddler-height clothesline.

STEPS

1. Demonstrate how to use clothespins to hang laundry on the clothesline, and allow your toddler time to practice.

2. Move only the laundry basket with laundry to the other side of the yard. Have your child do the laundry line relay by running to the basket, grabbing a piece of laundry, then running back to the clothesline and hanging the laundry up, repeating this until all items are on the line.

TIP *Try using a timer to see how fast your toddler can hang all the laundry. Invite one of your child's friends over for a race to see who can finish hanging their laundry first.*

CAUTION! *Supervise your toddler during play, and never leave the activity set up when not supervising, as the materials used can be a strangulation or injury hazard.*

Speedy Simon Says

This superfast version of the classic Simon Says game is a great way for older toddlers to practice listening skills and following directions. The fast pace of this game makes it best to play outside where you have plenty of space to move.

Messiness: 0
Prep Time: None
Activity Time: 15 minutes

MATERIALS

None!

STEPS

1. Come up with movements, like skip, run, gallop, shimmy, tiptoe, and march, then have your toddler practice each one.

2. Have him also practice changing the speed of the movements when you call out speed words like *fast, slow, faster,* and *slower.*

3. Explain the primary rule of Simon Says: Only follow commands that begin with "Simon says . . ." If he follows a command that didn't begin with it, he has to return to the starting point.

4. Take the role of "Simon" for the first round, then position yourself on the other side of the yard from your child. Call out speedy movement commands for your toddler to perform while moving toward you. Randomly start some commands with "Simon says . . ." and leave it off others.

5. The game is over when your toddler reaches you, or when the first person reaches you while playing with a group. That person gets to be "Simon" for the next round.

TIP *Make it more fun by switching out the name of "Simon" for a name or word related to your child's interests, favorite character, or a holiday, like "Elsa says . . ." "T-Rex says . . ." or "Lucky Leprechaun says. . . ."*

"X" Marks the Spot

On top of providing beneficial gross motor movement, this easy play idea provides excellent problem-solving practice.

Messiness: **2**
Prep Time: **5 minutes**
Activity Time: **20 minutes**

MATERIALS

Sidewalk chalk

Toys, such as cars, trucks, dolls, and blocks

Toy wagon

Pail

PREP

Use sidewalk chalk to draw a giant "X" on the pavement or sidewalk, then position a collection of toys about 20 or 30 feet from it. Make sure the wagon and pail are near the toys.

STEPS

1. Tell your toddler, "'X' marks the spot!" and challenge him to transfer all of the toys to the "X" as quickly as possible.

2. As your child begins transferring, likely carrying one toy at a time, encourage him to problem-solve by asking, "How can you make this hard job easier and faster?"

3. Allow him some time to problem-solve on his own, then prompt him to consider how the pail or wagon could help him. Encourage him to try using them.

4. After all of the toys are on the "X," have your toddler reflect by asking questions like, "What are the different ways you moved the toys?" "Which way was the easiest?" or "Did the pail or wagon make the job easier? Why do you think that is?"

Chalk Town Roadway

Sneak in some creativity for yourself by drawing sidewalk chalk art your toddler can play in!

Messiness: 3
Prep Time: None
Activity Time: 20 minutes

MATERIALS

Sidewalk chalk

Toy cars and trucks

STEPS

1. Use sidewalk chalk to draw a toy-car-size roadway using parallel lines on the pavement or sidewalk. If space allows, make it a large circular roadway with space in the middle for your child to sit in to play. If not, a long roadway along a sidewalk would work, too.

2. Invite your toddler to tell you things she would like along her roadway, such as a hospital, a farm, or a lake. Draw them while she plays cars on the roadway.

3. Encourage language development, as well as color and shape practice, by asking questions while you draw, such as "What else do you usually see at a park?" "What shape might the hospital be?" or "What color should we make this house?"

4. Allow your toddler plenty of free play time with her toy cars and trucks on her new chalk town roadway.

TIP *Don't worry about drawing perfectly. Just use basic shapes, simple lines, and lots of imagination. Your toddler will think you're the best artist in their tiny town!*

SKILLS
LEARNED

gross
motor skills

colors

sorting

visual
spatial skills

Hide & Seek Color Sort

Take some ball pit balls outside for this color-sorting spin on hide-and-seek.

Messiness: 1
Prep Time: None
Activity Time: 20 minutes

MATERIALS

Medium plastic bins, one per ball color

Construction paper, one sheet in each ball color

Ball pit balls, of various colors

STEPS

1. Line the bins up and have your toddler place a sheet of paper in each one, making a matching bin for each ball color.

2. Have him cover his eyes while you hide the balls around the yard.

3. Invite him to seek and find the balls, placing each one in its matching color bin.

Guess the Animal Yoga

Yoga is a great way for kids to develop body awareness, strengthen gross motor skills, and practice mindfulness. Doing animal-themed yoga outside offers the perfect environment for additional sensory input and extra-big movements.

Messiness: 0
Prep Time: None
Activity Time: 10 minutes

MATERIALS

None!

TIP *You can research "kids' animal yoga poses" online or at the library ahead of time. You can also find a link to some animal poses in the Resources section at the end of the book (page 149). Keep in mind, your toddler will have fun whether your animal poses are true yoga poses or ones you've simply made up.*

STEPS

1. Invite your toddler to sit crisscross in the grass. Help her calm her mind and body by asking her to notice what she is seeing, hearing, and feeling.

2. Demonstrate an animal yoga pose, including the animal's sounds. Have your toddler try to guess the animal, then copy your movements and sounds. Repeat, with different animals. Here are some to try:

    - **Cat or Tiger:** Get into a crawling position, then arch your back while meowing or roaring.
    - **Snake:** Lie flat on your belly with legs and feet together, arms outstretched, and hands together. Slowly move your hands and arms back and forth, while hissing.
    - **Bird:** Standing tall and straight, reach and stretch your arms out like wings. Slowly move your upper body and arms in a gliding or flying motion while chirping or cawing.
    - **Frog or Toad:** Squat down, and position your elbows on your knees while ribbiting or croaking.

Snowy Shape Freeze Dance

Bundle up and head outdoors on a snowy day for some creative freeze dancing and shape learning!

Messiness: 2
Prep Time: None
Activity Time: 15 minutes

MATERIALS

Snow

Music

STEPS

1. Have your toddler choose a shape, then follow you while you walk through the snow, making a giant shape with your footprints.

2. Randomly play and stop music while you have your child dance around the shape path and freeze in place each time the music stops.

3. Encourage her to use her arms and body while dancing, and giggle with her at the silly poses she ends up freezing in.

TIP *Play winter-themed songs to add to the seasonal fun.*

Alphabet Sweep

Combine letter learning and life skills practice with this outdoor active play idea.

Messiness: 2
Prep Time: 5 minutes
Activity Time: 20 minutes

MATERIALS

Sidewalk chalk

Broom, either toy or regular

Plastic letter magnets

PREP

1. Draw a large circle on the pavement with sidewalk chalk.

2. Randomly scatter the letter magnets on the pavement outside the circle.

STEPS

1. Have your toddler use the broom to sweep the letters into the circle.

2. Encourage him to call out the letters as he sweeps them into the circle.

3. Add to the challenge by calling out letters for him to locate and sweep into the circle.

Noisy Animal Tag

This silly spin on the classic game of tag is sure to inspire lots of smiles and laughter. The game is especially fun with a group of children.

Messiness: 0
Prep Time: **None**
Activity Time: **10 minutes**

MATERIALS

None!

STEPS

1. Help your toddler practice various animal sounds, then choose one to start the game.

2. Play the role of the noisy animal, making the sounds of your chosen animal as you chase and try to tag another player. When you tag someone, assign her an animal so she can play the role of the noisy animal and try to tag someone. Repeat, until each player gets a turn to be the noisy animal.

gross
motor skills

visual
spatial skills

numbers
and counting
1 2 3

SKILLS
LEARNED

Number Bucket Ball

A small soft ball makes this simple toss game toddler-friendly and fine to play anywhere. It's smart to play outdoors since toddler tosses can sometimes be unwieldy.

Messiness: 1
Prep Time: 5 minutes
Activity Time: 10 minutes

MATERIALS

3 to 5 large plastic buckets or bins

Dry-erase marker

Small soft ball

PREP

Use the dry-erase marker to label the side of each bucket with a number, starting with number 1 and counting up, then line them up in order.

STEPS

1. Have your toddler stand a few feet away and toss the ball into one of the buckets.

2. Encourage him to call out the number on the bucket while retrieving the ball.

3. Repeat, until he gets the ball in each bucket.

4. Make the game more fun and challenging by calling out numbers for him to aim for.

TIP *The dry-erase marker should easily wipe off plastic buckets after play, but test it on a small spot to be sure. Try sticky notes to label the buckets if you don't want to use the marker.*

SKILLS
LEARNED

gross
motor skills

language
development

listening

early literacy

Stop & Go Traffic Control

This ride-on-toy activity is fantastic for your toddler to practice listening and following rules. Plus, the homemade road sign offers exposure to words in his everyday environment.

Messiness: 2
Prep Time: 10 minutes
Activity Time: 30 minutes

MATERIALS

Red and green construction paper

Glue stick

9-by-12-inch piece of cardboard

Scissors

Black marker

Ride-on toys

Whistle

Sidewalk chalk (optional)

Small notebook and pen (optional)

Play road cones (optional)

STEPS

1. Have your toddler help glue red construction paper onto one side of a piece of cardboard and green construction paper onto the other side.

2. Cut the paper-covered cardboard into an octagon or circle shape. (Find a link to an octagon template in the Resources section, page 149.)

3. Use the marker to write "STOP" on the red side of the sign and "GO" on the green side. Read the words to your toddler and explain how the sign tells people what to do to stay safe. Explain how red means "STOP" and green means "GO."

4. Get out the ride-on toys and have your toddler come up with simple traffic laws to follow, such as "Stop when you see the red 'STOP' sign; go when you see the green 'GO' sign; and slow down when you hear the whistle."

5. Direct traffic while your child takes a joyride on his ride-on toy of choice.

TIP *Enhance play by trying the following:*

- *Draw road lines and parking spaces with sidewalk chalk.*
- *Issue traffic tickets using a paper pad and pencil.*
- *Set up cones to direct specific traffic patterns.*

CAUTION! *This activity is best in safe paved play spaces. If you're using a low-use parking lot or driveway, block off the area with bright play cones. Supervise your toddler during play, and never leave the activity set up when not supervising, as the materials used can be a strangulation or injury hazard.*

SKILLS
LEARNED

gross
motor skills

problem-
solving

memory

Backyard Obstacle Course

The ultimate outdoor kids' activity has to be an obstacle course, and these simple tricks using everyday backyard items make it easy to create one your toddler will love.

Messiness: 2
Prep Time: 10 minutes
Activity Time: 20 minutes

MATERIALS

Logs, boards, and/or wood blocks

String

Swing set

Ladder

Picnic table

Rope

Sticks

Plastic buckets

Timer (optional)

PREP

Set up an obstacle course using materials from around your home and yard. Try one of these easy ideas:

- **Stepping Logs:** Place logs on the ground, close together and in a row, for stepping on.
- **Swing-Set Spiderweb:** Wind and tie string around the posts of a swing set to make a spiderweb for crawling through.
- **Stepladder:** Lay a ladder flat on the ground for stepping between rungs.
- **Picnic Table Crawl or Climb:** Set up a picnic table for climbing over or crawling under.
- **Not-So-Tight Rope:** Position a rope in a wavy line on the ground for stepping along.
- **Jumping Sticks:** Lay large sticks on the ground for jumping over.
- **Balance Board:** Prop ends of a board up on short blocks for using as a balance beam.
- **Bucket Run:** Position buckets upside down a few feet apart for running around and weaving between.

1. Allow your toddler to follow your lead and practice each obstacle, giving each a name as you go.

2. Have your toddler try the obstacle course on her own. Prompt her with the names of each obstacle as she goes. Stay close by to offer a hand for assistance and safety.

3. Add to the excitement by timing your toddler with a stopwatch.

TIP *Adjust the number of obstacles for the age and ability of your toddler. Keep it to three or so obstacles for younger toddlers, and add more for older children.*

CAUTION! *Check all obstacles carefully prior to play, ensuring they are stable and free of sharp edges. Supervise your toddler during play, and never leave the activity set up when not supervising, as the materials used can be a strangulation or injury hazard.*

SKILLS
LEARNED | gross
motor skills | visual
spatial skills | sensory
development

Sandy Beach Obstacle Course

Set up a playful obstacle course right on the beach when you're on vacation. It's as simple as drawing a line in the sand!

Messiness: 3
Prep Time: 5 minutes
Activity Time: 10 minutes

MATERIALS

Stick

Sandy beach

Stopwatch (optional)

PREP

Use a stick to draw an obstacle course in the sand with some of the following ideas:

- Draw a series of lines in a row to jump over.
- Draw a long wavy line to walk along.
- Draw a straight line to use as a balance beam.
- Draw a spiral as a spot for standing and spinning in place.
- Draw circles for hopping from one to another.

STEPS

1. Demonstrate each obstacle for your child, then allow him to run the obstacle course.

2. Offer verbal assistance, as needed, and lots of cheering.

3. Add to the fun by timing him with a stopwatch.

CAUTION! *Keep your toddler away from sharp objects. If you're concerned about stick safety, draw in the sand with your foot instead.*

"How Low Can You Go?"

Set up an outdoor limbo party using just two lawn chairs and some colorful streamers. Your toddler will love moving and stretching her body in ways she never has before!

Messiness: 1
Prep Time: 5 minutes
Activity Time: 10 minutes

MATERIALS

2 lawn chairs

Crepe paper streamers

Masking tape
(optional)

PREP

1. Position the lawn chairs a few feet apart, backs to one another.

2. Tie or tape a length of crepe paper streamer from one chair to the other.

STEPS

1. Have your toddler arch her body back to limbo under the streamer. Tell her to try not to touch or rip the streamer, but if the streamer rips, just replace it.

2. Repeat, lowering the streamer a bit each time, to see how low your child can go.

3. Add lively music and encourage dancing during your limbo fun.

TIP *No crepe paper streamers? Try some ribbon, a broom handle, or a foam swim noodle.*

CAUTION! *Supervise your toddler during play, and never leave the activity set up when not supervising, as the materials used can be a strangulation or injury hazard.*

SKILLS
LEARNED

gross
motor skills

numbers
and counting

123

Number Line Frog Hop

Many toddlers are still learning how to hop and jump, and this simple number line activity provides lots of frog-themed practice.

Messiness: 1
Prep Time: **None**
Activity Time: **15 minutes**

MATERIALS

Sidewalk chalk

STEPS

1. Draw a long line on the sidewalk. Have your toddler count from 1 to 10 while you write each number, about a foot apart, along the line.

2. Optionally, draw a green lily-pad shape around each number to enhance the frog-themed imaginative play. (Find a link to a template in the Resources section on page 149, if needed.)

3. Invite your toddler to hop from number to number along the line. Challenge her to say each number and "Ribbit!" as she hops.

4. Have her practice counting down from 10 to 1 while hopping, too.

Giant Shapes Memory

The giant size of this memory game makes it great for playing outside. Just make sure it's not too windy, or your game pieces might blow away!

Messiness: 0
Prep Time: None
Activity Time: 15 minutes

MATERIALS

8 to 12 paper plates

Markers

STEPS

1. Have your toddler name the basic shapes, such as circle, square, triangle, and rectangle, as you draw each shape on 2 paper plates.

2. Randomly place the plates, shapes up, on the ground.

3. Call out a shape for your toddler to find. Challenge him to find its match.

4. Make the game more challenging by flipping the plates over, shapes down, and playing like a traditional memory game, where your toddler flips two over at a time to find matches.

Windy Day Play

Some lightweight scarves and a hula hoop make for excellent open-ended play on a windy day.

Messiness: 0
Prep Time: None
Activity Time: 15 minutes

MATERIALS

Lightweight scarves

Hula hoop

STEPS

1. Start by asking your toddler questions like "Do you think it is windy today? How do you know?" "Can you feel the wind?" and "How can we find out what direction the wind is blowing?" Provide the scarves and hula hoop for free play in the wind.

2. Hold the hoop upright, then have your toddler try to let a scarf go in the wind so it blows through the hoop. Challenge her to try moving the hoop to catch a scarf as you release it in the wind.

TIP *Find lightweight scarves at thrift stores and yard sales.*

- 4 -
EMBRACE NATURE

It's so much fun to explore the world alongside a toddler. Parenting my kids through their curiosity-filled toddler years truly enhanced my appreciation for the world around me. They helped me notice all the beautiful tiny things that I too often passed right by.

The following outdoor activities harness your toddler's intense curiosity for exploring the natural world around them. They offer incredible sensory experiences by using primarily natural materials, like leaves of all shapes and sizes, blades of glossy grass, bumpy pine cones from the backyard tree, smooth stones, and rough rocks.

Seeds of Mindfulness Sensory Bottles

Sensory bottles are great for inspiring mindfulness. The weight provides calming sensory input, while the contents offer something to focus on. Making these outside gives your toddler an opportunity to examine seeds without any worry about messes.

Messiness: **4**
Prep Time: **None**
Activity Time: **15**

MATERIALS

4 or more packets of seeds

4 small bowls

Magnifying glass (optional)

4 (8-ounce) empty clear plastic water bottles

Vegetable oil

Funnel (optional)

Craft glue

Clear packing tape

CAUTION! *This activity may not be suitable for children who put objects in their mouths during play.*

STEPS

1. Invite your toddler to inspect the seed packets and identify the plants pictured on them. Open each packet and dump the seeds into separate bowls for your toddler to explore. Allow your toddler to use a magnifying glass to get a closer look.

2. Explain the science of seeds, saying something like, "When seeds are planted or dropped to the ground, they use the soil, water, and sunlight to help them grow into plants, flowers, fruits, and vegetables. See how the different plants have different seeds?"

3. Using a funnel, fill each plastic bottle, until almost full, with oil. Allow your toddler to help put one type of seed in each bottle. Add some glue around the lid threads before tightening it on the bottle. Use clear packing tape to attach the seed packets to their coordinating seed bottles.

4. Show your child how to shake the bottles to watch the seeds inside float and fall down.

TIP *Offer a sensory bottle to your child when she needs to calm her mind or body.*

Funny Nature Faces

Get creative arranging natural objects into silly faces, then boost your toddler's language development and oral motor skills by telling stories about them in funny voices.

Messiness: 3
Prep Time: None
Activity Time: 10 minutes

MATERIALS

Small objects from nature, like bark, leaves, twigs, acorns, rocks, or moss

Basket

STEPS

1. Take your toddler on a hunt for small natural objects, collecting them in the basket.

2. Show your child how to arrange the objects into a silly face, such as using pebbles for eyes, a leaf for a mouth, acorns for cheeks, and bark for hair. Give your silly face a name, then tell a story in a funny voice about this nature person.

3. Invite your toddler to make his own silly face out of the natural objects. Help him come up with a silly name and story for his nature person, too.

CAUTION! *Monitor your toddler closely when playing with small natural objects. This activity may not be suitable for children who put objects in their mouths during play.*

Magical Nature Wand

Use this sticky trick on your next family hike or park visit to help your toddler start her very own nature collection.

Messiness: 3
Prep Time: None
Activity Time: 20 minutes

MATERIALS

Double-sided tape

Wooden paint
stir stick

Small natural objects

STEPS

1. Apply double-sided tape to both sides of the stick, leaving an unsticky handle at one end.

2. Invite your toddler on a hunt for small natural objects to stick to her wand. Tell her the natural materials give the wand its magic.

3. Encourage magical pretend play with her new sticky nature wand, such as pretending the wand helps her locate and observe animals or transforms her into a woodland fairy.

CAUTION! *Monitor your child closely as the materials used can be a choking hazard. Also, review rules for stick safety, such as, "The wand is only magical with slow movements," "wands are never for tapping or poking people," "always walk when holding the wand," and "running makes it lose its magic."*

Squishy Stone Tower Challenge

Challenge your toddler to some sensory play and problem-solving using simply stones and playdough.

Messiness: 4
Prep Time: None
Activity Time: 20 minutes

MATERIALS

Playdough
(recipe on page 27, or store-bought)

10 or more stones

Measuring tape or ruler (optional)

STEPS

1. Allow your toddler free play time with the play-dough and stones.

2. Encourage him to try squishing playdough between the rocks to stack and build with them.

3. Challenge him to build the tallest tower he can. If possible, help him measure his towers with a measuring tape or ruler.

CAUTION! *Although the homemade playdough is taste-safe, it is not fully edible.*

SKILLS
LEARNED
sensory
development
fine
motor skills
memory
visual
spatial skills

Leaf Rubbing Match

Leaf rubbing is one of those classic nature activities most of us probably remember from our own childhoods. Share in this memory with your toddler while you work together to make a nature-themed matching game.

Messiness: 3
Prep Time: None
Activity Time: 20 minutes

MATERIALS

5 leaves

Double-sided tape

10 pieces of paper

Crayons, with
labels removed

STEPS

1. Have your toddler choose a leaf and help her tape it onto a piece of paper.

2. Position another piece of paper on top and help hold it while your toddler rubs the side of a crayon all over it. Share in her excitement when she sees the shape and texture of the leaf underneath emerge in the crayon rubbing. Let her examine the leaf and the leaf rubbing side by side.

3. Repeat, until you have a leaf paper and a matching crayon rubbing for each leaf.

4. Have your toddler close her eyes while you randomly arrange the papers, faceup. Have her open her eyes, choose one leaf, and find its matching crayon rubbing. Set the match aside and have her repeat, until all matching pairs have been found.

5. Challenge her further by randomly arranging the papers facedown, and then playing like a traditional memory game.

Crayon Nature Color Hunt

Help your toddler see all of the beautiful colors in the natural world around her with this simple color hunt activity and DIY color book.

Messiness: 1
Prep Time: None
Activity Time: 20 minutes

MATERIALS

6- or 8-count box of crayons

Smartphone camera (optional)

4-by-6 photo paper and printer (optional)

4-by-6 mini photo album (optional)

STEPS

1. Grab a box of crayons and head outside for a color hunt!

2. Have your child choose a crayon from the box, then find an item of that color in nature. If possible, take a closeup photo of the crayon near its matching color in nature.

3. Repeat with each crayon color in the box.

4. If you took photos, have them printed and add them to a mini photo album to make your toddler her very own book of nature colors.

Peanut Butter Birdseed Castle

Encourage observation and appreciation of our feathered friends with this sensory-rich bird feeder craft.

Messiness: **4**
Prep Time: **5 minutes**
Activity Time: **20 minutes**

MATERIALS

Cardboard egg carton

Scissors

Twine

4 or more cups birdseed

Medium plastic bin

1 (16-ounce) container peanut butter

Small spatula or spreading knife

Ice cream cones, various types

Pine cones

PREP

1. Cut the top off the egg carton and discard. Punch a hole in each corner of the carton and tie a three-foot length of twine to each one.

2. Place the bird seed in a bin.

STEPS

1. Together, use a spatula to spread peanut butter on the outside of ice cream cones and pine cones, then roll them in the bin of birdseed to coat them.

2. Use peanut butter like glue to stick the birdseed-coated cones upside down onto the egg carton, making it look like a castle.

3. Add more peanut butter and birdseed to cover the entire castle.

4. Help your child hang the bird feeder castle where he can watch the birds enjoy their royal treat.

TIP *If your child has an allergy to peanuts, use sunflower seed butter or lard instead.*

CAUTION! *Make sure your toddler understands that none of the bird feeder materials are edible while crafting with them. This activity may not be suitable for children who put objects in their mouths during play. Keep your toddler away from sharp objects.*

SKILLS
LEARNED

sensory
development

social-emotional
development

mindfulness

Calming Sensory Sit

Teach your toddler a valuable mindfulness strategy with this simple sensory sit right in your backyard.

Messiness: 1
Prep Time: **None**
Activity Time: **5 minutes**

MATERIALS

None

STEPS

1. Sit crisscross together on the grass.

2. Have your child put one hand on his belly and one on his heart, then take three deep breaths. Tell him this will help calm his body and mind.

3. Ask your toddler to notice what his body is sensing by asking what he is seeing, hearing, smelling, and feeling.

TIP *If your toddler is wiggly, try having him sit on your lap. Or try similar mindfulness questions while going on a nature walk.*

| fine motor skills | shapes and letters | sensory development | early literacy | SKILLS LEARNED |

Sandbox Name Rocks

Give your toddler a head start on learning how to spell her name with some simple-to-make letter rocks and sandbox play.

Messiness: **4**
Prep Time: **10 minutes**
Activity Time: **10 minutes**

MATERIALS

Smooth flat rocks, one per letter in your child's name

Paint marker or permanent marker

Sandbox

PREP

Write each letter of your child's name on a separate rock.

STEPS

1. Write your child's name in the sand with your finger.

2. Have your child place each letter rock below its matching letter in the sand.

3. Challenge her by arranging the name rocks in the sand, then have her use her finger to write each letter below its matching stone with her finger.

SKILLS
LEARNED   science   visual   sensory   fine
                        spatial skills   development   motor skills

Polka-Dot Pizza Garden

Most toddlers love playing in the dirt. Add some hands-on learning by helping your toddler plant her very own container garden full of pizza ingredients.

Messiness: **4**
Prep Time: **None**
Activity Time: **20 minutes**

MATERIALS

Potting soil

Large terra-cotta pot

Pizza ingredient seeds, such as tomatoes, basil, bell peppers, and oregano

4 craft sticks

Permanent marker

Watering can with water

Acrylic paint, in white, red, and green

3 paper plates

3 cotton balls

3 clothespins

STEPS

1. Have your toddler help fill the pot with potting soil.

2. Divide the top of the soil into four equal sections by drawing a large "X" in it with your finger.

3. Help your child plant a different type of seed in each section of soil. Follow the directions on the seed packets.

4. Write each plant name on a craft stick to use as simple plant markers.

5. Have your toddler water the newly planted seeds.

6. Make sure the outside of the pot is clean and dry. Squirt a different color of paint onto each paper plate. Make a dabber for each paint color by pinching a cotton ball inside the end of a clothespin. Have your child use the dabbers to dab white, red, and green polka dots all over the outside of the pot. Allow to dry.

CAUTION! *Monitor your child closely as the materials used can be a choking hazard. This activity may not be suitable for children who put objects in their mouths during play.*

SKILLS
LEARNED

sensory
development

fine
motor skills

science

visual
spatial skills

Nature Impressions Puzzle

Take some playdough outside to help your child explore the types of textures found in nature. Squishing and pressing playdough is great work for hand muscles.

Messiness: 3
Prep Time: None
Activity Time: 15 minutes

MATERIALS

Small objects from nature, such as leaves, bark, stones, acorns, or pine cones

Playdough
(recipe on page 27, or store-bought)

Rolling pin (optional)

STEPS

1. Help your child flatten the playdough to about an inch thick.

2. Invite him to examine the feel of each object, then press each object into the playdough, leaving impressions in it.

3. Have your toddler match each object to its impression in the playdough puzzle.

CAUTION! *Although the homemade playdough is taste-safe, it is not fully edible.*

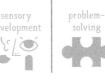

Touch & Feel Guessing Game

Nature is so full of unique and interesting textures. Help your toddler explore the wonders of all of them with this easy touch-and-feel-box activity.

Messiness: 3
Prep Time: None
Activity Time: 20 minutes

MATERIALS

Small objects from nature, such as leaves, bark, stones, acorns, or pine cones

Empty tissue box

STEPS

1. Place the natural objects into the tissue box.

2. Have your toddler reach into the hole in the top of the box and feel one of the natural objects. Make sure she doesn't pull it out or peek at it.

3. Ask your toddler to describe what she is feeling, encouraging the use of descriptive words, such as *smooth, bumpy, hard, rough, scratchy,* and *small.*

4. Have her try to guess what the object is, then have her pull it out to see.

5. Repeat until your toddler has examined each object.

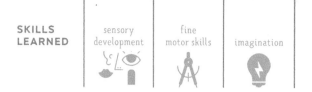

Nature Confetti

There's something so soothing about the soft, slippery feel of green leaves and grass. Invite your toddler to explore them while also getting valuable fine motor and scissors skill practice.

Messiness: 2
Prep Time: None
Activity Time: 15 minutes

MATERIALS

Grass

Leaves

Medium plastic bin

Kids' safety scissors (optional)

Dolls or animal toys

STEPS

1. Invite your toddler to hunt for grass and leaves, collecting some in a plastic bin.

2. Have him tear the grass and leaves into little pieces. Or let him snip them with scissors to practice his cutting skills.

3. Sprinkle the leaves and grass confetti at a pretend doll or animal toy celebration.

CAUTION! *Make sure your toddler sprinkles the confetti down onto his toy celebration and not up into his eyes.*

Calming Snow Spiral

Take advantage of a serene winter snow cover to teach your toddler the calming benefits of movement and mindfulness.

Messiness: 2
Prep Time: 10 minutes
Activity Time: 15 minutes

MATERIALS

Snow

Snow shovel

PREP

1. Use a snow shovel to clear a circular area, just large enough for two people to comfortably stand in.

2. Shovel a walking path spiraling out from the circle.

STEPS

1. Invite your toddler to join you as you slowly and quietly walk the spiral path toward the center circle.

2. As you walk together, encourage mindfulness by asking your toddler what she is sensing, using questions like, "What are your ears hearing?" "What is your nose smelling?" and "What does your skin feel?"

3. Once you reach the center circle, take a moment to share a warm, tight hug before starting your calm, quiet walk back out, along the path.

TIP *No snow? Try one of these other ways to make a calming spiral path:*

- *Draw a spiral path with sidewalk chalk on pavement.*
- *Use a stick to draw a spiral path in the sand at the beach.*
- *Arrange your garden hose into a large spiral on the lawn.*
- *Sprinkle flour out of a coffee can to make a spiral line in the grass.*

SEASONAL ACTIVITY

Paint Chip Flower Sort

Grab some paint chips the next time you're at the store for some flower-filled color sorting.

Messiness: 2
Prep Time: None
Activity Time: 20 minutes

MATERIALS

Flowers

Basket

Paint chips

STEPS

1. Have your toddler go on a hunt for flowers, collecting some in a basket.

2. Arrange various paint chips on a flat surface, then challenge your toddler to sort the flowers, placing each by its matching-color paint chip.

TIP *Be careful of where you pick flowers. Many public locations and parks prohibit it. If you don't have many flowers to pick at home, consider purchasing an inexpensive bouquet from the supermarket for this activity.*

Critter Hunt & Count

My toddlers were always fascinated by anything creepy and crawly. Help your toddler find and count critters in his own backyard!

Messiness: **2**
Prep Time: **None**
Activity Time: **15 minutes**

MATERIALS

Notebook

Marker

Magnifying glass
(optional)

STEPS

1. Invite your toddler to join you on an adventure to find and count critters.

2. Make it challenging by giving him specific things to find, such as:

   - an animal with a tail
   - the color yellow
   - something with wings
   - a critter with more than 4 legs

3. Each time he spots a critter, have him draw a tally mark on a notebook page. (Use the printable via the link in the Resources section on page 149, if you prefer.)

4. After you've completed your adventure, help him count the tally marks to see how many critters he found.

CAUTION! *Never allow your toddler to touch creatures unless you are absolutely certain they are not poisonous or harmful.*

SKILLS
LEARNED

sensory
development

science

creativity

Picnic Table Nature Collage

Using clear sticky contact paper on a kid-size picnic table is a fun way to entice your toddler to explore natural materials and dabble in collage-making.

Messiness: 3
Prep Time: 5 minutes
Activity Time: 20 minutes

MATERIALS

Roll of clear
contact paper

Masking tape

Kid's picnic table
or small plastic
outdoor table

Small objects from
nature, such as leaves,
grass, moss, and bark

Medium plastic bin
(optional)

PREP

Tape contact paper, sticky-side up, along the entire length of your child's picnic table.

STEPS

1. Have your toddler explore the new sticky texture on her picnic table.

2. Invite her to find and stick natural materials on it.

3. Let her get lots of exercise by running back and forth, finding and sticking one item at a time onto the contact paper. Or give her a plastic bin so she can collect a bunch of materials at once.

sensory
development

fine
motor skills

SKILLS
LEARNED

Dandelion Sensory Bag

I know those dandelions in the yard can seem like a nuisance, but they become the star of this nature-themed sensory bag.

Messiness: 3
Prep Time: None
Activity Time: 20 minutes

MATERIALS

Dandelions

Basket

Permanent marker

Gallon-size plastic zip-top bag

1 (16- to 20-ounce) bottle clear hair gel

Duct tape

STEPS

1. Have your toddler collect dandelions and dandelion leaves in a basket.

2. Use a permanent marker to draw a large circle on a zip-top bag. Hold the bag open while your toddler puts the dandelions and dandelion leaves inside.

3. Help your toddler fill the bag with hair gel.

4. Zip the bag closed and lay it flat to see if it contains enough gel to make it squishy for little fingers. Add more if needed. Zip the bag closed and fold duct tape over the zip-top edge.

5. Place the sensory bag on a flat surface, circle side up. Invite your toddler to poke and squish at the dandelions inside to move them into the circle.

| gross motor skills | sensory development | shapes and letters | visual spatial skills |

Leaf & Letter Swim

I bet most toddlers would love to play in a kiddie pool filled with leaves. Add even more fun and learning with some foam alphabet toys.

Messiness: **4**
Prep Time: **10 minutes**
Activity Time: **20 minutes**

MATERIALS

Kiddie pool

Fallen leaves

Foam bath letter toys

PREP

Fill your child's kiddie pool with fallen leaves, then mix in the foam bath letters.

STEPS

1. Invite your toddler to take a leaf swim in her kiddie pool.

2. Have her dig through the leaves to find the foam letters. Help her name each one as she finds it.

3. Add to the challenge by calling out specific letters for her to find in the leaves.

CAUTION! *If you live in an area where ticks are prevalent, check your child's body for ticks after leaf play.*

Petal Dough Play

Make some nature-filled and texture-rich playdough using wildflowers your toddler collects from around the yard or park.

Messiness: **4**
Prep Time: **None**
Activity Time: **20 minutes**

MATERIALS

Flowers

Basket

Playdough
(recipe on page 27, or store-bought)

Large plastic tray or baking sheet pan (optional)

STEPS

1. Invite your toddler on a hunt to find flowers, picking and collecting some in a basket.

2. Have him pluck the petals from the flowers and place them on a tray.

3. Offer the playdough for him to explore with the petals on the tray. Encourage him to press petals into the playdough to make patterns and designs. Or have him knead some of the petals right into the playdough.

4. Allow your toddler lots of time for free play, exploring and creating with the petals and playdough.

CAUTION! *Although the homemade playdough is taste-safe, it is not fully edible. This activity may not be suitable for children who put objects in their mouths during play.*

Googly-Eyed Nature Friends

Add a little silliness to your outdoor play by letting your toddler add googly eyes to natural objects around the yard.

Messiness: 3
Prep Time: None
Activity Time: 10 minutes

MATERIALS

Large plastic tray or baking sheet pan (optional)

Objects from nature, such as pine cones, shells, stones, sticks, and leaves

Self-adhesive googly eyes, various sizes and colors

White glue (optional)

STEPS

1. Offer your toddler a tray of natural objects or have him join you on a hunt to collect some.

2. Invite him to stick the googly eyes onto the objects to make them come alive.

3. Help him make up silly names and stories about his new nature friends.

TIP *If the adhesive on your googly eyes isn't strong enough, use glue to adhere them.*

CAUTION! *Monitor your child closely as the materials used can be a choking hazard. Make sure sticks have dull ends for safe play, and do not let unsteady toddlers walk or run with them.*

- 5 -
GET WET!

What better way to make memories with your toddler on a hot day than with some lively outdoor water play? From spraying siblings with the hose to splishing and splashing in the kiddie pool, water play is a staple of childhood—and for good reason. Not only is it a fun way to cool off when the temperature rises, but water play also offers endless benefits to a toddler's developing sensory system and motor skills.

sensory
development

fine
motor skills

colors

visual
spatial skills

Jiggly Stars & Fish Swim

Did you try Jiggly Gelatin Shapes (page 39) from chapter 2? This toddler water activity takes the jiggly fun even further, right into your toddler's kiddie pool!

Messiness: 5
Prep Time: 20 minutes +
4 hours refrigeration time
Activity Time: 20 minutes

MATERIALS

5 cups boiling water

Mixing bowl and measuring cup

Whisk

2 (0.6-ounce) boxes sugar-free flavored gelatin, 1 blue and 1 yellow

4 envelopes (1 tablespoon each) unflavored gelatin

Cooking spray

2 (13-by-9-inch) baking pans

Star and fish cookie cutters

Spatula

Large plastic food storage container (optional)

Kiddie pool with water

1. Pour 2½ cups of boiling water into a mixing bowl. Stir and dissolve 1 box of flavored gelatin and 2 envelopes of unflavored gelatin into the water in the bowl. Pour the mixture into a cooking spray-coated baking pan. Repeat with the remaining ingredients. Refrigerate both pans for 4 hours, or until set.

2. Place the bottom of each pan in warm water for 15 seconds to loosen the gelatin. Use the cookie cutters to cut fish shapes out of the blue gelatin and star shapes out of the yellow gelatin. Carefully transfer the gelatin stars and fish into a food storage container; cover and refrigerate until playtime.

STEPS

1. Add the gelatin stars and fish to a water-filled kiddie pool. Invite your toddler to swim with the jiggly stars and fish!

2. Challenge her to try to catch the slippery gelatin stars and fish with her hands.

3. Help your toddler identify the colors of the stars and fish as she catches them.

CAUTION! *Keep your toddler away from the stove and hot ingredients. Monitor your child closely as the materials used can be a choking hazard. Consider cutting the leftover gelatin scraps into bite-size pieces to have on hand for safe snacking. Always supervise your toddler closely around water.*

SKILLS
LEARNED | fine
motor skills | shapes
and letters | visual
spatial skills

Magic Letters Spray Game

Grab those plastic letter magnets off the fridge and head outside for some wet letter learning!

Messiness: 2
Prep Time: None
Activity Time: 15 minutes

MATERIALS

Plastic letter magnets

Small spray bottle

Water

STEPS

1. Ask your toddler to randomly place the letter magnets on the sidewalk.

2. Have him use the spray bottle to mist water over the letters, thoroughly wetting the sidewalk around them. Help him squeeze the trigger, if necessary.

3. Have him move the letter magnets to reveal the dry magic letters underneath.

4. Call out letters for your little one to spray with water. Help him locate the letters if needed.

Swish & Squeeze Laundry

Boys and girls alike will love the soapy fun and whimsy of this toddler-size laundry activity.

Messiness: 3
Prep Time: 5 minutes
Activity Time: 20 minutes

MATERIALS

Rope

Kids' body wash

2 plastic buckets

Doll clothes, wash-cloths, or socks

Plastic laundry basket

Clothespins

PREP

1. Tie some rope between two trees, poles, or lawn chairs to create a toddler-height clothesline.

2. Add a squirt of kids' body wash to one bucket. Add water to both.

STEPS

1. Help your toddler gather some toddler-size laundry, such as doll clothes, washcloths, or socks, in a laundry basket.

2. Have him wash each article of laundry in the soapy water, swish in the plain water to get the soap out, squeeze to wring the water out, and use clothespins to hang on the clothesline.

3. Practice counting each article of laundry as he hangs them on the clothesline.

CAUTION! *Always supervise your toddler closely around water. Supervise your toddler during play, and never leave the activity set up when not supervising, as the materials used can be a strangulation or injury hazard.*

fine
motor skills

visual
spatial skills

science

Spray & Roll Beach Ball Soccer

Every kid loves to get their hands on the hose! This activity gives them the chance while also providing motor skills practice and even some experience with the science of force and motion.

Messiness: 3
Prep Time: None
Activity Time: 20 minutes

MATERIALS

Hose with water

Beach ball or
lightweight ball

Plastic laundry basket
or large plastic bin

STEPS

1. Show your toddler how to squirt the hose at the beach ball, making it move with the force of the water.

2. Place a laundry basket on its side across the yard, and challenge your toddler to use the hose and the force of the spraying water to roll the ball into the basket.

TIP *No hose? No worries. Try using a forceful squirting toy instead.*

Sink or Float Toy Sort

Introduce the simple science of sinking and floating with your toddler's toys.

Messiness: 3
Prep Time: None
Activity Time: 20 minutes

MATERIALS

Water

Large plastic bin

Water-friendly toys

Permanent marker

Masking tape

2 plastic trays

STEPS

1. Add water to a bin, and add one toy you know will sink and one you know will float. Explain the difference using simple terms like, "Objects sink if their tiny parts, called molecules, are close together. Objects float if their molecules are farther apart, allowing air between them. The air helps them float."

2. Use a marker and masking tape to label one tray with an "S" for SINK and the other with an "F" for FLOAT. Have your toddler place each toy you just tested on its appropriate tray.

3. Help your toddler gather water-friendly toys and test each one in the water to see which ones sink or float. Have her place each toy on the appropriate "SINK" or "FLOAT" tray based on the results of her experiment.

CAUTION! *Always supervise your toddler closely around water.*

SKILLS
LEARNED

visual
spatial skills

problem-
solving

sensory
development

science

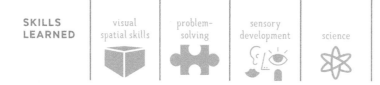

Waterfall Fence

No need for an expensive store-bought waterfall toy when you've got plenty of free parts right in your recycling bin.

Messiness: 4
Prep Time: 20 minutes
Activity Time: 20 minutes

MATERIALS

Heavy-duty scissors or utility knife

Empty plastic water bottles

Electrical tape, various colors

Cable ties or staple gun and staples

Fence

Large plastic bin

Plastic cup

Water

PREP

1. Use the scissors to cut each bottle in one of the following ways: a straight cut to cut off the bottom, a diagonal cut to cut the bottom off at a slant, or a lengthwise cut to cut it entirely in half. Poke holes through the plastic opposite the cut openings of some of the bottles to allow for water dripping and trickling.

2. Fold electrical tape over any sharp plastic edges on the bottles. Consider using different colors of tape on different bottles to increase the potential for color learning during play.

3. Use cable ties wrapped around the bottles or threaded through holes poked in them to attach the bottles to the fence, each with the cut opening upward, positioned above another bottle, and angled, so that when water is poured into a top bottle, it will flow downward and fall into another bottle, and then downward again, into another bottle, and so on. Your toddler should be able to reach the top bottle.

4. Position a large bin on the ground underneath the waterfall fence. Fill it with water and add a cup for scooping.

STEPS

1. Have your toddler use the cup to scoop water from the bin on the ground, pour it into a bottle at the top of the waterfall fence, then watch it flow downward through various bottles to return to the bin.

2. Allow her lots of free play time experimenting and learning firsthand about gravity and motion with her new waterfall fence.

TIP *If you want a waterfall fence you can move or store when not in use, make one on a wood pallet or large piece of lattice trellis.*

CAUTION! *Keep your toddler away from sharp objects. Always supervise your toddler closely around water.*

Animal Sailboats

Sailing toy boats is a classic play activity every kid should experience. Add to the sensory fun and fine motor skills practice by making your own toy boats!

Messiness: 3
Prep Time: None
Activity Time: 20 minutes

MATERIALS

Aluminum foil

2 to 4 plastic food storage containers, various sizes

Large plastic bin

Water

Small plastic animal toys

STEPS

1. Fold a long piece of aluminum foil until it's about 8 to 12 inches square and has a few layers.

2. Have your toddler smooth the square of foil over an upside-down container to make a boat shape. Carefully remove the formed foil and fold or crumple the edges, if necessary, to reinforce the boat's shape.

3. Repeat, using various containers to make different size boats.

4. Fill a large bin with water and invite your toddler to sail the boats in it.

5. Give her some plastic toy animals to take for rides in the boats. Encourage her to experiment and count how many animals she can sail in the boats.

CAUTION! *Always supervise your toddler closely around water.*

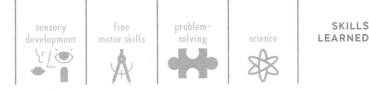

Ice Animal Rescue

This sensory-rich play activity is perfect for cooling off outside on a hot summer day. It inspires lots of problem-solving and even some science learning, too.

Messiness: 3
Prep Time: 5 minutes +
6 hours freezing time
Activity Time: 20 minutes

MATERIALS

Small plastic
animal toys

Large plastic food
storage container

Water

Wooden spoon

Small bowl of salt

Pitcher of warm water

PREP

Add plastic animal toys to a large food storage container. Fill it with water and place it in the freezer for about 6 hours, or until fully frozen.

STEPS

1. Remove the ice block from the container, and challenge your toddler to rescue the animals inside the ice. Give her time for problem-solving and experimenting with the wooden spoon, salt, and warm water for the rescue.

2. Encourage your toddler to observe how the ice is affected when she chips at it with the wooden spoon, sprinkles it with salt, and pours warm water on it. Ask which method is easiest and helps melt the ice fastest.

TIP *If you have trouble getting the ice out of the container, dip the container in warm water to loosen the ice.*

SKILLS LEARNED	fine motor skills	gross motor skills	sensory development	science	creativity

Rainy-Day Marker Run

Don't let a little rain keep you from getting creative with your toddler outdoors. In fact, use the rain for some splashy art inspiration!

Messiness: **4**
Prep Time: **None**
Activity Time: **20 minutes**

MATERIALS

Watercolor paper or other heavyweight paper

Washable markers

Rain

STEPS

1. Before you go outside, ask your toddler to color a sky on a piece of paper with markers. Discuss colors she has seen in the sky and encourage her to cover the entire paper in marker.

2. Put your toddler in her rain gear. Have her hold the paper in front of her with outstretched arms, marker-side facing up. On the count of three, have her run a lap or two in the rain around the yard, keeping the paper in front of her, marker facing up, before returning to the house.

3. Encourage her to notice how the raindrops affected the marker sky, making the colors bleed and blend to look like a rainy-day sky. Lay the art flat to dry.

TIP *If the rain is too light, or it isn't raining at all, give your toddler a spray bottle to dampen her marker art instead.*

SKILLS
LEARNED

gross
motor skills

social-emotional
development

visual
spatial skills

sensory
development

Family Beach-Pail Relay

What better place for water play than the beach? Get the entire family involved with this water relay competition—a perfect activity for your sandy vacation!

Messiness: **4**
Prep Time: **None**
Activity Time: **20 minutes**

MATERIALS

4 to 6 beach pails

2 plastic cups

Water

STEPS

1. Divide your family into two teams. Each team should position a set of 2 or 3 beach pails in the sand, about 3 feet away from one another, but the same distance from the ocean. Give each team a plastic cup.

2. Explain the object of the game: to be the first team to fill their pail with ocean water using just the cup.

3. To play the game, one person from each team runs to the ocean's edge with the cup, fills the cup with ocean water, then holds it upright over his head while running back and dumping any water remaining in the cup into his team's pails. Another person does the same, and so on, until all of their pails are full.

CAUTION! *Have one adult stationed at the ocean to help little ones fill their cups safely. Or use a big bin of water instead of the ocean's edge. Always supervise your toddler closely around water.*

Lucky-Seven Sprinkler Run

Add some learning to sprinkler play with a little game of counting.

Messiness: **4**
Prep Time: **None**
Activity Time: **20 minutes**

MATERIALS

2 dice

Small, clear plastic food storage container

Sprinkler

Hose with water

STEPS

1. Place the dice inside a small clear container and tightly secure the lid. Have your toddler shake the container and look through the bottom to see the number on the dice. Help her count the dots, if necessary.

2. If the number on the dice is lucky number seven, she should run through the sprinkler seven times. If the number is any other number, she should run once through the sprinkler after counting up to that number.

3. Repeat, for lots of counting and sprinkler fun!

Will It Hold Water?

Raid the house for containers that can hold water, then offer some open-ended play time for exploring size, space, and volume.

Messiness: 3
Prep Time: None
Activity Time: 20 minutes

MATERIALS

Containers, such as cups, ladles, pitchers, pans, colanders, measuring cups, wire baskets, small trash cans

Large plastic bin

Water

STEPS

1. Go on a hunt around the house for various containers that might hold water, collecting them in a large bin as you go. Let your toddler collect any container, as long as it's water-friendly, even if you know it won't hold water. This will allow her to experiment and learn through play.

2. Go outside and dump the containers out on the grass, then fill the bin with water.

3. Have your toddler test each container by scooping water from the bin, then sorting the containers on each side of the bin, based on whether each holds water or not.

4. Together, compare the size and volume of the containers, asking questions like, "Which container is the biggest?" "Which is the smallest?" "Which do you think holds the most water? Which holds the least?" and "Why doesn't this container hold water?"

5. Have her pour water from the biggest container into the smallest, then from the smallest into the biggest to see what happens. Challenge her to put the containers in order from smallest to largest.

CAUTION! *Always supervise your toddler closely around water.*

Car Wash ABCs

The memories of helping my parents wash the family car, with the soap scent from the big sudsy sponges and the cold mist of the spraying hose, are as vivid as yesterday. Try this easy alphabet activity the next time you wash your car for some sudsy memories with your toddler.

Messiness: **4**
Prep Time: **None**
Activity Time: **20 minutes**

MATERIALS

Window markers, or erasable liquid chalk markers

Car windows, or outside house window

Hose with water

Stepstool or large plastic bin (optional)

Large sponges

Plastic bucket of soapy water

STEPS

1. Practice saying the alphabet with your toddler as you use the window marker to write each letter on the windows of your car.

2. Call out random letters for your child to find and spray with water from the hose. Or provide a bucket of soapy water and a sponge for him to use to wash the letters off. Help him safely stand on a stepstool or upside-down bin to reach, if necessary.

3. Encourage your toddler to say the letters as he washes them.

TIP *Not up for a car wash? Try a window alphabet wash on the outside of a house window your toddler can reach instead.*

CAUTION! *Always supervise your toddler closely around water. Choose a soap that is nontoxic and kid-friendly, and be sure to test soap and markers on a small area of your vehicle prior to use. Also, remain close by and assist to prevent falls if he needs to stand on a stepstool or bin.*

SKILLS
LEARNED

fine
motor skills

language
development

visual
spatial skills

Follow the Water-Line Leader

Introduce your toddler to the fascinating science of water absorption and evaporation right on the sidewalk on a warm summer day.

Messiness: 3
Prep Time: None
Activity Time: 10 minutes

MATERIALS

Large paintbrush

Water

Plastic cup

STEPS

1. Have your toddler use a paintbrush dipped in a cup of water to paint different types of water lines on the sidewalk. Help her describe them, using words like *long, short, big, small, straight, wiggly, curvy, zigzag, jagged, dotted,* and *dashed.*

2. Invite her to play a "follow the water-line leader" game by watching you paint different types of lines, then painting her own matching water lines. Switch roles and let your toddler be the leader for the next round.

3. Encourage your toddler to notice the way the water lines disappear as the water evaporates. Explain the science in a simple way, such as "Where did your line go? It disappeared! The sunshine and warm day made the water on the sidewalk dry up and evaporate into the air and clouds."

CAUTION! *Always supervise your toddler closely around water.*

sensory development	gross motor skills	language development	listening	SKILLS LEARNED

Sing, Stomp & Splash!

Toddlers just seem to be attracted to puddles. Embrace the puddle-pull on a rainy day with a popular kids' song and some wet-stomping fun!

Messiness: 5
Prep Time: None
Activity Time: 10 minutes

MATERIALS

Rain boots

Puddles

STEPS

1. Teach your toddler a rainy-day version of the classic song, "If You're Happy and You Know It":

   *If it's rainy and you know it, stomp and splash! (*stomp*stomp*)*

   *If it's rainy and you know it, stomp and splash! (*stomp*stomp*)*

   If it's rainy and you know it, then you might as well enjoy it,

   *If it's rainy and you know it, stomp and splash! (*stomp*stomp*)*

2. Get your rain boots on, head outside, and find a puddle.

3. Demonstrate the activity by singing the first line, "*If it's rainy and you know it, stomp and splash!*" then stomping twice in the puddle, *(*stomp*stomp*)*, instead of clapping.

4. Invite your toddler to practice once with you, then join you in singing the entire song, stomping in the puddle when prompted.

SKILLS
LEARNED
sensory
development
fine
motor skills
colors
sorting

Pom-Pom Squish & Sort

Fuzzy little pom-poms are fun to explore with water since they soak it up and become squishy (and a little messy) for little fingers. All that water-squishing makes this messy activity best to do outdoors.

Messiness: 3
Prep Time: None
Activity Time: 15 minutes

MATERIALS

Water

Medium plastic bin

Pom-poms, in various colors

Empty clear plastic water bottles, one per pom-pom color

STEPS

1. Add a few inches of water to the bin, then have your toddler add the pom-poms. Allow him to explore and squish them with his hands.

2. Demonstrate pom-pom squishing and color sorting by using your finger to push a wet pom-pom of a different color into each bottle. Have your toddler squish and sort the rest of the pom-poms into the bottles, using the colored pom-pom inside each bottle as a guide.

CAUTION! *Always supervise your toddler closely around water. This activity may not be suitable for children who put objects in their mouths during play.*

Floating Faces

Inspire imagination and creativity in the kiddie pool with this easy DIY idea using a popular kids' craft material.

Messiness: **4**
Prep Time: **10 minutes**
Activity Time: **20 minutes**

MATERIALS

Permanent marker

Craft foam sheets, around 4-by-6-inch

Scissors

Kiddie pool

Water

CAUTION! *Always supervise your toddler closely around water.*

PREP

1. Use a permanent marker to draw one facial feature on each rectangle of foam. Make a wide variety and each one unique, such as an eye with long lashes, a big circular eye, a long pointy nose, a round plump nose, a nose with big nostrils, a pointy elf-like left ear, a giant lumpy left ear, a right ear with an earring, smiling plump lips, tiny pointed lips, or a mouth sticking its tongue out. (Find a link to examples in the Resources section on page 149.)

2. Keep them rectangular or use scissors to trim around each facial feature, making each a unique shape.

STEPS

1. Fill the kiddie pool with water and invite your toddler to take a swim.

2. Float the foam facial feature pieces in the pool and encourage your toddler to move and arrange them on the surface of the water to make silly faces. Practice naming the facial features (nose, eyes, ears, etc.) while doing so.

3. Help her make up silly stories inspired by the faces she makes.

TIP *No kiddie pool? Float and arrange the foam facial feature pieces in a large shallow bin of water instead.*

Swing-Set Car Wash

Here's a simple version of the elaborate DIY kiddie car washes you might have seen online, using the swing set right in your backyard.

Messiness: **4**
Prep Time: **20 minutes**
Activity Time: **20 minutes**

MATERIALS

Swing set or playset

Scissors

2 to 4 old towels

Cable ties or
duct tape

Serrated knife

5 to 10 foam pool
noodles

String or twine

Hose and sprinkler
with water

Water-friendly
ride-on toys

PREP

1. Unhook and remove the swings from the top bar of the swing set.

2. Cut wide strips in the length of a towel, leaving about 6 inches at one end intact so the strips stay together. Use cable ties to attach the intact end of the towel to the top bar of the swing set, allowing the strips to hang down. Repeat with more towels until the entire width of one swinging spot has hanging towel strips for the car wash.

3. Carefully use the knife to cut a hole through the end of a pool noodle. Use string, threaded through the hole, to tie the pool noodle to the top bar of the swing set so it hangs down. Repeat, hanging pool noodles side by side along the bar for an entire swinging spot width.

1. Position the sprinkler so it sprays the entire swing-set car wash.

2. Invite your toddler to ride water-friendly ride-on toys through the car wash, letting the hanging wet towel strips and pool noodles slide over him.

TIP *You can try this using any monkey bars or high bar on an outdoor playset. If you don't have a swing set or playset, try hanging the items from a strong clothesline.*

CAUTION! *Keep your toddler away from sharp objects. Supervise your toddler during play, and never leave the activity set up when not supervising, as the materials used can be a strangulation or injury hazard.*

Sidewalk Rainbow Bingo

Here's a fun outdoor version of a favorite classic game, bingo, but with a wet spin!

Messiness: 4
Prep Time: 5 minutes
Activity Time: 20 minutes

MATERIALS

Sidewalk chalk in red, orange, yellow, green, blue, purple

Empty tissue box

Plastic bucket

Water

Large sponge

PREP

1. Draw a large circle on the sidewalk with each color of chalk, lined up in the order of the rainbow: *red, orange, yellow, green, blue,* and *purple.* Place the pieces of chalk in an empty tissue box.

2. Fill a bucket with water, and add the sponge.

STEPS

1. Have your toddler reach into the tissue box, pull out a piece of chalk, and identify the color.

2. Ask her to find the matching-color circle on the sidewalk and toss a wet sponge at it. If she hits the circle, she should set that piece of chalk aside. If she doesn't, she must return that piece of chalk to the box. Retrieve the sponge and place it back in the bucket.

3. Repeat until your child hits each color of the rainbow and can yell, "Rainbow bingo!"

CAUTION! *Always supervise your toddler closely around water.*

Sheet Shape Color Squirt

Grab some water-squirting toys for some shape learning your toddler is sure to remember!

Messiness: 3
Prep Time: 10 minutes
Activity Time: 20 minutes

MATERIALS

Black permanent marker

Old white sheet

Water

Food coloring, in various colors

Water-squirting toys

PREP

1. Use a permanent marker to draw large basic shapes on a white sheet. Hang the sheet from a fence or swing-set bar. Alternatively, you could lay it flat on a clean area of ground.

2. Add water and a few drops of food coloring to a squirting toy, then close it and shake it up to color the water. Repeat, filling each water-squirting toy with a different color of water.

STEPS

1. Invite your toddler to use the squirting toys to spray the shapes on the sheet.

2. Make it more challenging by calling out shapes for her to squirt or even colors to squirt at specific shapes.

CAUTION! *Make sure your toddler knows never to squirt at other people, especially since the water contains food coloring.*

Colorful Ice Fishing

Fishing for colorful ice cubes is a great way to cool off on a hot day, while also getting color learning and hand-eye coordination practice.

Messiness: 4
Prep Time: 10 minutes + 6 hours freezing time
Activity Time: 20 minutes

MATERIALS

Water

Food coloring, in the primary colors of red, yellow, and blue

Plastic pitcher

3 ice cube trays

Gallon-size plastic zip-top bags

Kiddie pool

Hose with water

Small fishing net (optional)

3 medium plastic food storage containers (optional)

PREP

1. Add 2 cups of water and a few drops of food coloring to a pitcher, then stir. Pour the colored water into an ice cube tray. Repeat, using a different color of water for each tray. Place the trays in the freezer for 6 hours, or until frozen.

2. Pop the colorful ice cubes out of the trays and store them in large zip-top bags in the freezer until playtime.

STEPS

1. Fill the kiddie pool with water, then add the colored ice cubes.

2. Invite your toddler to sit at the edge of the pool and go ice fishing using a small fishing net to scoop the ice cubes out of the water.

3. Encourage your child to name the colors as she catches them. Add more challenge by calling out a specific color for her to catch.

4. If you have containers, have her sort the ice cubes into them by color.

TIP *No fishing net? Your toddler could also use a plastic cup or simply her hands to scoop out ice cubes. If you don't have a kiddie pool, try this activity in a large plastic bin of water instead.*

CAUTION! *Always supervise your toddler closely around water.*

- 6 -
OUTDOOR ART

Taking art-making outdoors is the perfect solution for toddlers still perfecting motor skills and exploring the world through their senses. Outside, your toddler can be free to investigate new art materials and explore creatively without worry over the mess. The sensory-rich natural world around him is bound to enhance the creativity and learning.

Let this lower-stress environment inspire low-stress child-led creativity, too. Keep your focus on curiosity, creativity, fun, and learning during your toddler's outdoor art-making versus how the finished art or craft might look. Doing so will help your toddler gain the most educational and developmental benefits from each of the artsy activities in this chapter while also expanding his appreciation for art and creativity.

SKILLS
LEARNED

oral motor
development

sensory
development

creativity

colors

BIG Bubbly Box

Bubble painting is a fun way to explore with color while also getting in some beneficial oral motor work and sensory regulation.

Messiness: **4**
Prep Time: **10 minutes**
Activity Time: **20 minutes**

MATERIALS

Small plastic food storage containers, one per color

Bubble solution

Food coloring, in various colors

Straws

Rubber bands

Large cardboard box

TIP *Cut windows and doors into the fully dry bubble-painted box to transform it into a simple playhouse, dollhouse, or toy car garage for imaginative play.*

PREP

1. Fill each container about halfway with bubble solution, then turn each a different color by stirring in about 10 drops of food coloring per container.

2. Bundle up 3 to 5 straws, with ends even, using a rubber band to hold them together. Repeat, making and placing a straw bundle in each container of bubble solution.

3. Place a large cardboard box upside down on the ground and the containers with straw bundles near one another on the ground.

STEPS

1. Invite your toddler to blow colorful bubbles all over the top and sides of the box by dipping the end of a straw bundle in bubble solution, pointing it at the box, and blowing through the other end. Have her repeat with each color of bubble solution until the box is covered in colorful bubbles. (Add more food coloring, as needed, to ensure bright bubble prints on the box.)

2. Inspire color learning by calling out bubble colors for your child to pop with her finger. Allow lots of free bubble-painting time, then leave the box in the sunshine to dry.

Swing-Paint a Rainbow

Kids have an innate need to swing, spin, and hang upside down. These movements help develop and regulate their vestibular sensory system, the one controlling their sense of body awareness and balance. Try this unusual painting technique to get some of that beneficial movement in while painting a colorful rainbow.

Messiness: 5
Prep Time: 10 minutes
Activity Time: 15 minutes

MATERIALS

6 squeeze bottles

Washable paint in red, orange, yellow, green, blue, and purple

Large piece of cardboard

Toddler swing

CAUTION! *Make sure your toddler is safely secured in the swing so she can focus on squirting the paint. Supervise your toddler during play, and never leave the activity set up when not supervising, as the materials used can be a strangulation or injury hazard.*

PREP

1. Fill the squeeze bottles each with a different color of paint. If needed, add some water and shake to make the paint thin enough to squirt.

2. Place a sheet of cardboard on the ground underneath your toddler's swing.

STEPS

1. Secure your toddler in her toddler swing. Help her identify the first color in the rainbow (red) and give her the red squeeze bottle.

2. Give her swing a gentle push, and have her squirt the red paint downward, painting red lines along with the motion of the swing.

3. Stop the swing. Repeat the swing-painting process with the next color of the rainbow, and so on, until your toddler has swing-painted each color of the rainbow on the cardboard. Let the cardboard dry in the sunshine.

TIP *Find squeeze bottles right in your recycling bin! Use cleaned-out clear ketchup, salad dressing, and other condiment bottles.*

SKILLS
LEARNED

gross motor skills

visual spatial skills

colors

patterns

creativity

Backyard Yarn Art

Ever see a tree, park bench, or light pole adorned with colorful knitted yarn? If so, you've experienced yarn bombing, the quirky street-art-installation trend intended to add color, pattern, and creativity to our everyday environment. Invite your toddler to create some color- and pattern-filled yarn art right in your own backyard.

Messiness: **2**
Prep Time: **None**
Activity Time: **15 minutes**

MATERIALS

Large outdoor object, such as a tree, swing-set pole, or fence

Balls of yarn, in various colors

Tape (optional)

Scissors

STEPS

1. Explain to your toddler that he will help you make an outdoor art installation by wrapping colorful yarn around something in the yard, like a tree, swing-set pole, or fence. Let him choose the object to use.

2. Have him pick a ball of yarn and help him tie or tape the yarn end to the chosen object. Have him wrap the yarn around the object by either holding the yarn and walking around the object or standing on the opposite side of the object and passing the yarn ball back and forth to you while it unravels. Use scissors, as needed, to cut the yarn.

3. Let him choose another color of yarn and repeat, wrapping it next to the first color.

4. Add some simple pattern learning by using the yarn colors to make an AB pattern (red, orange, red, orange . . .) or an AAB pattern (red, red, orange, red, red, orange . . .).

TIP *Keep this outdoor art project in your own backyard unless you have permission from the property owner to do an art installation on location.*

CAUTION! *Keep your toddler away from sharp objects.*

Magic Glitter Wand

Doesn't it seem like all kids are drawn to glitter? When you give in to using glitter with your toddler, you inevitably end up finding shimmers of it everywhere. This magical craft is a great way to satisfy your toddler's desire for sparkle while keeping the mess outside.

Messiness: 5
Prep Time: **None**
Activity Time: **15 minutes**

MATERIALS

Stick

Paintbrush

Small bowl of white glue

Glitter

STEPS

1. Invite your toddler to hunt for a stick to transform into a magic glitter wand.

2. Have him paint stripes of glue onto the stick, leaving a few inches at one end glue-free for a handle.

3. Help him sprinkle glitter onto the glue on the stick, maybe even making patterns with different colors of glitter. Let the stick dry fully in the sunshine.

4. Show your child how to discover the magical powers of the stick. For example, maybe the wand makes people he points to make the animal sound he assigns them. Or it may have special abilities to help him count the animals he sees in his backyard.

CAUTION! *Review some rules for safe magic glitter wand play: the wand is only magical with slow movements; never tap or poke people; no running with the wand.*

Monster Truck Slide & Paint

Have you ever had your toddler paint with toy cars and trucks? It's fun, but not as exciting as painting with toy monster trucks sliding down a slide!

Messiness: 5
Prep Time: None
Activity Time: 20 minutes

MATERIALS

Masking tape

White paper

Slide

Washable paint

Monster truck toys

STEPS

1. Use tape to attach slightly overlapping sheets of white paper along the entire length of the slide. Squirt paint along the paper at the top of the slide.

2. Place monster truck toys at the top of the slide, then help your toddler climb the ladder and stand toward the top so he can reach the trucks and see down the slide. Stay nearby for safety.

3. Have him push the monster truck toys down the slide so they roll through the paint, leaving tire tracks along the paper as they go. Repeat, adding more paint as needed.

4. Carefully remove the tire-track-painted papers, and set aside or hang on the clothesline to dry. Let your toddler use the tracks as roads for playing with the trucks.

CAUTION! *Supervise your toddler during play, and never leave the activity set up when not supervising, as the materials used can be a strangulation or injury hazard.*

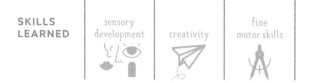

Painted-Ice Printmaking

This cool art project is perfect for outdoor creativity on a hot day as well as a great introduction to simple printmaking.

Messiness: **4**
Prep Time: **10 minutes +
6 hours freezing time**
Activity Time: **10 minutes**

MATERIALS

Water

9-by-13-inch
baking pan

Washable paint

Paintbrushes

Watercolor
paper or other
heavyweight paper

PREP

Pour a few inches of water into a baking pan, then put the pan in the freezer for around 6 hours, or until the water is fully frozen.

STEPS

1. Pop the ice block out of the pan, onto the ground. (Dip the pan in warm water to loosen the ice, if needed.) Invite your toddler to paint on the ice block.

2. Help her press a piece of paper onto the top of the ice block, rub her hands all over the top of the paper, then lift the paper to reveal the ice paint print.

3. Rinse the paint off the ice block with water and repeat to make another ice paint print.

TIP *Use a holiday-themed or character-shaped baking pan to make an ice block to paint. If you're painting on an outdoor table instead of on the ground, place an old dish towel under the ice block to keep it from sliding around.*

colors

shapes
and letters

fine
motor skills

SKILLS
LEARNED

Snowy Squirt-Painted Shapes

This winter art activity offers excellent fine motor skill practice and basic shape learning.

Messiness: **4**
Prep Time: **5 minutes**
Activity Time: **20 minutes**

MATERIALS

Squeeze bottles

Water

Food coloring

Stick or broom

Snow

PREP

1. Fill a squeeze bottle with water and a few drops of food coloring. Close and shake the bottle to distribute the color. Repeat with as many bottles as you have, filling each with a different color.

2. Use a long stick to draw large basic shapes in the snow.

STEPS

1. Have your toddler use the squeeze bottles to color in the shapes in the snow.

2. Make it more challenging by calling out certain shapes to paint and colors to use.

TIP *Find squeeze bottles right in your recycling bin! Use cleaned-out clear ketchup, salad dressing, and other condiment bottles.*

Sidewalk Chalk Pattern Quilt

Explore patterns with your toddler with a giant quilt design right on the sidewalk.

Messiness: **4**
Prep Time: **None**
Activity Time: **15 minutes**

MATERIALS

Sidewalk chalk

STEPS

1. Use sidewalk chalk to draw a giant rectangular grid of squares on the sidewalk.

2. Have your toddler help fill each square with a different sidewalk chalk pattern, like polka dots, dashed lines, wiggly lines, diagonal lines, small triangles, numbers, or letters.

TIP *Look at the patterns on a real quilt for inspiration before heading outside.*

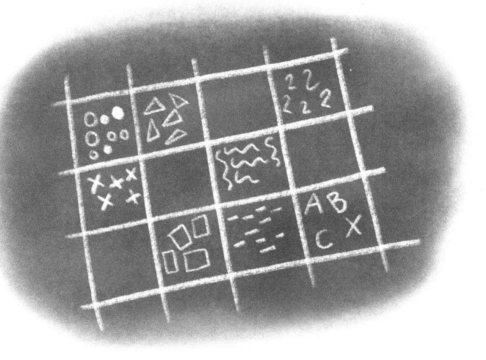

Sticker-Painted Flowerpot

This easy outdoor toddler craft would be a special gift for Grandma, a daycare provider, or just for you to keep.

Messiness: 4
Prep Time: None
Activity Time: 20 minutes

MATERIALS

Heart or star stickers

Terra-cotta flowerpot

Acrylic paint

Paper plate

Small round sponges

STEPS

1. Have your toddler randomly place stickers on the outside of a terra-cotta pot.

2. Give her a few colors of paint on a paper plate, along with some sponges. Have her dab paint all over the outside of the pot, covering the stickers. Leave the pot to dry fully.

3. Help her peel the stickers off to reveal paint-free shapes where the stickers were.

Windy Day Streamers

Don't forget about performance art when you're getting creative outside with your toddler. This colorful craft makes the perfect performance prop on a windy day. Using the natural element of wind opens up the opportunity for some weather and science learning, too.

Messiness: 3
Prep Time: 5 minutes
Activity Time: 20 minutes

MATERIALS

Scissors

Ribbon and crepe paper streamers

Cardboard paper tube

Double-sided tape or white glue

Stapler and staples

Duct tape

PREP

1. Cut the ribbon and paper streamers into two-foot-long pieces.

2. Line the inside of each end of the cardboard tube with double-sided tape or white glue.

STEPS

1. Have your toddler place the ends of the ribbons and streamers onto the sticky tape inside each end of the tube. Squeeze one end of the tube flat, sandwiching the streamer ends inside (while leaving the rest of the streamers outside the tube), and staple two or three times to hold it that way. Apply duct tape around it to cover the staples. Repeat with the other end of the tube.

2. Have your child play with his new wind streamers in the wind, running, dancing, and waving it creatively.

SKILLS
LEARNED

fine
motor skills

colors

science

visual
spatial skills

Sidewalk Fizzing Squirt

This colorful fizzing fun will so enthrall your little one, he'll barely notice the fine motor work his little hands are doing.

Messiness: **4**
Prep Time: **None**
Activity Time: **10 minutes**

MATERIALS

3 small plastic food storage containers

White vinegar

Food coloring, in red, yellow, and blue

Baking soda

Various medicine droppers

STEPS

1. Fill each container with white vinegar and have your toddler add a few drops of food coloring to each, tighten the lids on, and shake each one to create different colors of vinegar. Help him identify each color while doing so.

2. Sprinkle baking soda in a circle shape on the sidewalk. Show your toddler how to use the various droppers to suck up the colored vinegar, then squirt it on the baking soda circle. Watch the excitement as the color fizzes and bubbles.

3. Give him time to squirt the different primary colors of vinegar onto the baking soda circle. Encourage him to notice how the fizzing colors mix to make new colors when they get close to one another.

Color Mixing Made Fun!

Introduce basic color mixing to your toddler with this simple activity.

Messiness: **4**
Prep Time: **None**
Activity Time: **20 minutes**

MATERIALS

1½ cups cornstarch

1½ cups water

Mixing bowl

Whisk

6 squeeze bottles

Funnel

Food coloring, in primary colors: red, yellow, and blue

STEPS

1. Measure the cornstarch and water and have your toddler add them to the mixing bowl. Help her use a whisk to stir until the ingredients are combined and without lumps. Add more cornstarch or water, if needed, to adjust the consistency to be squirtable.

2. Distribute this mixture evenly among 3 squeeze bottles using a funnel. Have your toddler add 5 to 10 drops of each food coloring to each bottle of paint mixture. Secure the lids, then have her shake them to distribute the coloring.

3. Have her squirt equal parts of red and yellow paint into an empty bottle. Secure the lid and let her shake it to make the paint turn orange. Repeat, using yellow and blue paint to make green, and blue and red paint to make purple.

4. Give your toddler the paint-filled squeeze bottles to squirt some colorful creations on the sidewalk.

Flower Heart Suncatcher

Invite your toddler on a hunt for colorful flowers, then use the petals for this sweet heart-shaped suncatcher.

Messiness: 3
Prep Time: 5 minutes
Activity Time: 10 minutes

MATERIALS

Scissors

Clear contact paper

Construction paper

Tape

Flowers

Basket

PREP

1. Cut two pieces of clear contact paper the same size as the construction paper. Tape one onto a flat outdoor surface, sticky-side up, with the paper backing removed. Set the other piece aside.

2. Fold a piece of construction paper in half lengthwise, then cut a large half-heart from the fold, so that when you unfold the paper, it will have a heart cut out of the center.

3. Position this paper onto the sticky contact paper. There should be sticky contact paper showing through the heart cutout.

STEPS

1. Invite your toddler to go on a flower hunt around the yard, picking and collecting various flowers in a basket.

2. Have her bring the flower collection to the craft area, then pluck the flower petals and place them on the sticky heart inside the construction paper.

3. When the flower petal art is complete, place the other piece of clear contact paper, backing removed and sticky-side down, on top, sandwiching the flower petal art inside.

4. Remove the suncatcher art from the table and trim the edges to an inch or so larger than the heart. Help your toddler tape the suncatcher to a window.

SKILLS
LEARNED

gross
motor skills

shapes
and letters

visual
spatial skills

science

Sidewalk Shape Shadows

This creative outdoor activity gets your little one exploring the basic science of light and shadows, while also learning basic shapes.

Messiness: 2
Prep Time: 5 minutes
Activity Time: 20 minutes

MATERIALS

Scissors

Construction paper

Sunshine!

Sidewalk chalk

STEPS

1. Have your toddler try to name the basic shapes as you cut each one, large, out of a piece of paper.

2. Show him how to hold a paper shape up in the sunlight to cast a shape shadow on the sidewalk. Show him how the shadow moves and the shape changes when he moves.

3. Have him stand still like a statue while you trace his shadow, including his shape shadow, on the sidewalk using sidewalk chalk. Repeat, with your child holding each paper shape. Ask your child to match the paper shapes to the corresponding shape shadow on the sidewalk.

Paint-Splatter Bug Swat

This fun and messy outdoor painting activity will have your toddler using both her fine motor and gross motor skills.

Messiness: 5
Prep Time: 5 minutes
Activity Time: 20 minutes

MATERIALS

Large white paper or poster board

Masking tape

Baking sheet pan

Washable paint

Bug stickers

Flyswatter

PREP

1. Tape a large piece of white paper on a fence or flat surface.

2. Place the sheet pan near the paper and squirt a few colors of paint on it.

STEPS

1. Have your toddler randomly stick the bug stickers onto the paper.

2. Invite her to dip a flyswatter in the paint on the pan and swat it at the bug stickers on the paper.

3. Get ready for splattering paint and giggles!

TIP *Simply draw bugs on the paper if you don't have bug stickers.*

Foamy Finger-Painting

Give finger-painting a unique feel with foil and shaving cream!

Messiness: 5
Prep Time: 5 minutes
Activity Time: 20 minutes

MATERIALS

Aluminum foil

Masking tape

Shaving cream

Washable paint, in two
or three colors

PREP

Wrap the top of the kids' picnic table or a large tray with foil. Use tape to secure it, if necessary.

STEPS

1. Invite your toddler to help squirt shaving cream all over the foil, then spread it out with his hands.

2. Squirt the finger paint, randomly, on the shaving cream, and let your toddler use his fingers to swirl it and make marks in it.

3. Encourage him to notice how the finger paint and shaving cream swirl together in a marbled effect. Challenge him to draw different types of lines in the foamy finger paint, such as wavy, zigzag, spiral, and straight.

4. Use the hose for easy cleanup.

Texture Touch Box Collage

Explore and celebrate nature's diverse textures with an easy toddler collage craft.

Messiness: **4**
Prep Time: **None**
Activity Time: **20 minutes**

MATERIALS

Various natural objects

Medium plastic bin

Shoebox lid, or other shallow cardboard box

White glue

Paintbrush

Squares of construction paper scraps

STEPS

1. Take your toddler on a hunt around the yard for natural objects of various textures, collecting them in a plastic bin as you go.

2. Explain what texture is by saying something like, "Texture is how something feels to the touch." Challenge your toddler to explain how each natural object feels as she finds it, using words like *bumpy, smooth, rough,* and *scratchy.*

3. Have your toddler paint the inside of the box with glue, then cover the glue with colorful construction paper squares.

4. Have her glue the various textured natural objects inside the box. Encourage her to use lots of glue, as it will dry clear. Allow the box collage to dry fully.

TIP *If you want to preserve your toddler's collage for display, but the objects loosen after the glue dries, reattach them using a hot glue gun. Just make sure to keep your toddler away from the glue gun while you work.*

CAUTION! *Monitor your child closely as the materials used can be a choking hazard.*

sensory
development

fine
motor skills

science

creativity

Leaf Ornaments

This messy clay craft gets your toddler exploring leaves and results in pretty keepsake ornaments.

Messiness: **4**
Prep Time: **None**
Activity Time: **20 minutes + drying time**

MATERIALS

Playdough
(recipe on page 27, or store-bought)

Baking sheet pan

Wax paper

Leaves

Skewer or straw

Oven (optional)

String

STEPS

1. Have your toddler roll a handful of dough into a small ball and place it on a baking sheet lined with wax paper. Show her how to place a leaf on top of the dough and squish both down using the palm of her hand. Have her peel the leaf off to see the detailed impression it left in the dough. Repeat, using various leaves, until all the dough has been used.

2. Use a straw to cut a hole in each ornament, then allow the ornaments to air-dry. You can also bake them in an oven set to 150°F for about 4 hours, or until fully dry. Check them occasionally during the drying process, and use a skewer or straw to reopen their holes, as needed.

3. Tie a loop of string onto each ornament for hanging.

TIP *Keep the dried ornaments natural or have your toddler paint them with acrylic paint once dry.*

CAUTION! *Although the homemade playdough is taste-safe, it is not fully edible.*

visual
spatial skills

fine
motor skills

creativity

SKILLS
LEARNED

Painted Stone Snake

Not only will your toddler love painting the stones, but he'll enjoy setting up his snake in his sandbox or your flower garden.

Messiness: **4**
Prep Time: **None**
Activity Time: **20 minutes**

MATERIALS

8 or more stones, smooth and clean

Acrylic paint, green

Paintbrush

Craft glue

Googly eyes

2-inch piece of red ribbon

STEPS

1. Join your toddler as he collects stones from your backyard or local park.

2. Invite him to paint the stones in various shades of green. Let them dry.

3. Have your toddler glue 2 googly eyes and a small piece of red ribbon (as the snake's tongue) on one of the stones. Let the glue dry.

4. Ask your toddler to arrange the painted stones in a snake pattern in his sandbox or in the flower bed for decoration.

Sensory Ball Shake Painting

This is the perfect outdoor art activity for wiggly toddlers to get moving and shaking while also creating art.

Messiness: **4**
Prep Time: **None**
Activity Time: **20 minutes**

MATERIALS

Tape

White paper

Large plastic bin, with tight lid

Washable paint

Spiky sensory balls

STEPS

1. Tape paper to the bottom of the plastic bin.

2. Let your toddler choose a few colors of paint, and help her squirt some of each onto the paper in the bin.

3. Invite her to explore the feeling of each sensory ball as she puts it in the bin. Encourage her to use descriptive words, such as *bumpy*, *spiky*, and *bristly*.

4. Have her tip and tilt the bin and watch the sensory balls roll back and forth through the paint, leaving paint trails on the paper.

5. Put the lid securely on the bin. Have her hold one end while you hold the other and *SHAKE* it.

6. Open the lid to see the textured shake painting on the paper. Remove it and allow to dry.

TIP *No spiky sensory balls? Use any washable plastic balls.*

Dough & Objects Sculptures

Offer lots of opportunity for sensory development and creativity with a simple setup of small objects and playdough. Keep this one outside where you won't have to worry about the playdough mess or small objects rolling under couches.

Messiness: **4**
Prep Time: **5 minutes**
Activity Time: **20 minutes**

MATERIALS

Small objects, such as bottle caps, small container lids, beads, letter magnets, pebbles, small blocks, or buttons

Large plastic divided tray

Playdough (recipe on page 27, or store-bought)

STEPS

1. Place different small objects in each part of the divided tray. Give your toddler the tray and some playdough.

2. Encourage her to sort through the loose parts. Talk about some things she might be able to build with the items.

3. As you begin to build together, explain the concept of sculpture using a simple statement like, "Sculpture is a type of art that takes up space, like a statue, and isn't just flat, like a drawing on paper."

4. Challenge her to make the tallest sculpture she can.

CAUTION! *Although the homemade playdough is taste-safe, it is not fully edible. This activity may not be suitable for children who put objects in their mouths during play.*

Resources

ACTIVITY PRINTABLES

Find printable resources at https://B-InspiredMama.com/outdoor-toddler-activities-resources for the following activities:

- Number Line Frog Hop (page 64)
- Guess the Animal Yoga (page 53)
- Stop & Go Traffic Control (page 58)
- Critter Hunt & Count (page 87)

CHILDREN'S BOOKS

Rain! by Linda Ashman and Christian Robinson

This little board book all about looking on the bright side of a rainy day would be perfect for accompanying the Rainy-Day Marker Run on page 106.

Outside Your Window: A First Book of Nature by Nicola Davies and Mark Hearld

The poetry in this book inspires toddlers and preschoolers to explore the natural wonders right outside their window. The rich mixed-media collage illustrations bring the natural elements being portrayed to life.

Breathe Like a Bear: 30 Mindful Moments for Kids to Feel Calm and Focused Anytime, Anywhere by Kira Willey and Anni Betts

This kid-friendly book about mindfulness includes simple breathing and movement exercises you can do with your child outdoors (or anywhere). Pair this with Guess the Animal Yoga on page 53.

Because of an Acorn by Lola M. Schaefer, Adam Schaefer, and Frann Preston-Gannon

Follow the journey of an acorn that grows into a tree but impacts far more in nature's magical circle of life. This book is perfect with the Seeds of Mindfulness Sensory Bottles on page 70.

Mrs. Peanuckle's Bug Alphabet by Mrs. Peanuckle and Jessie Ford

This sweet board book is full of collage-like illustrations taking toddlers through an alphabet adventure learning about bugs. It includes interactive prompts to make it even more exciting for little ones. It's one of a series of *Mrs. Peanuckle's Alphabet* books that each celebrate a different part of backyard nature, from vegetables to flowers to birds to trees.

Leaf Man by Lois Ehlert

This whimsical children's book about a "leaf man" and other leaf creations would be perfect to pair with the Funny Nature Faces on page 71.

Technicolor Treasure Hunt: Learn to Count with Nature by Hvass & Hannibal

This nature-inspired color hunt book would be ideal to read before heading out on the Crayon Nature Color Hunt on page 75.

RESOURCE BOOKS

Play & Learn Toddler Activities Book: 200+ Fun Activities for Early Learning by Angela Thayer

This awesome collection, written by my blogging-mama friend, Angela Thayer (of the blog *Teaching Mama*), is the book that inspired my book! Her focus on play that includes developmentally appropriate learning is spot-on.

A Little Bit of Dirt: 55+ Science and Art Activities to Reconnect Children with Nature by Asia Citro

Looking for more outdoor fun? You can't go wrong with *A Little Bit of Dirt*! You know it will be full of clever activities and ideas when it's written by Asia Citro, my longtime friend and blogger at *Fun at Home with Kids*, and author of multiple kids' activity books as well as the award-winning kids' chapter book series, *Zoey and Sassafras*.

The Slime Book by Stacey Garska Rodriguez and Jennifer Tammy Grossi

If your toddler likes the slime-making in this book (see page 25), grab *The Slime Book* for more ideas to keep him busy with sensory-beneficial slime-making. From edible and holiday versions to a slime you can draw on, *The Slime Book* has an oozy recipe for everyone and every occasion.

Let's Go Outside: Sticks and Stones - Nature Adventures, Games and Projects for Kids by Steph Scott and Katie Akers

This is the book for you if you're looking for even more inspiration for outdoor kids' activities. I love its emphasis on discovering and appreciating the magic of nature as well as its inclusion of nature facts and learning.

100 Fun & Easy Learning Games for Kids: Teach Reading, Writing, Math, and More with Fun Activities by Amanda Boyarshinov and Kim Vij

This book is full of clever games to make learning enjoyable. While it is geared slightly more for preschoolers, there are still plenty of letter- and number-learning activities you could use with your toddler.

Tinkerlab: A Hands-On Guide for Little Inventors by Rachelle Doorley

This book boasts 55 experiments for encouraging curiosity and creative problem-solving through "tinkering!" It's full of authentic hands-on learning ideas.

99 Fine Motor Ideas for Ages 1 to 5 (Volume 1) by various authors

So many great hands-on activities for little ones. Get your toddler strengthening those fine motor muscles with some of these busy bags, kids' crafts, DIY toys, and more.

Loose Parts 2: Inspiring Play with Infants and Toddlers (Loose Parts Series) by Lisa Daly and Miriam Beloglovsky

If your toddler liked the loose parts activities in this book (on page 147, for example), then definitely check out this book of loose play ideas. It breaks down the benefits and logistics of loose parts play with little ones and includes tons of inspiration.

BLOGS

Busy Toddler (blog) BusyToddler.com

Susie shares tons of quick and easy toddler activities with a focus on fun hands-on learning. She tries to ensure each activity has no prep or less than five minutes of prep so real moms can actually implement them.

Hands On As We Grow (blog) HandsOnAsWeGrow.com

Jamie Reimer has amassed an extensive resource for moms and kid-caregivers on her blog promoting hands-on play and learning activities. Not only does her blog have thousands of free ideas, but Jamie also offers helpful activity plans in the form of eBooks and through a monthly membership called *The Activity Room*.

Toddler Approved (blog) ToddlerApproved.com

Kristina aims for each activity to foster creativity and a love for learning during toddlerhood and beyond.

Teaching 2 and 3 Year Olds (blog) Teaching2and3YearOlds.com

Sheryl Cooper is a teacher of toddlers and preschoolers who shares all of her tried-and-tested early learning ideas on her blog. Her ideas aren't just for the classroom; they're simple enough for any busy mom to pull off.

Teaching Mama (blog) TeachingMama.org

Angela Thayer uses her years of teaching experience to develop fun learning activities toddlers and preschoolers love.

References

American Academy of Pediatrics. "Toddler." Accessed October 6, 2018. https://www.healthychildren.org/english/ages-stages/toddler/Pages/default.aspx.

Yogman, Michael, Andrew Garner, Jeffrey Hutchinson, Kathy Hirsh-Pasek, and Roberta Michnick Golinkoff. "The Power of Play: A Pediatric Role in Enhancing Development in Young Children." *Pediatrics.* Last modified September 1, 2018. Accessed October 6, 2018. http://pediatrics.aappublications.org/content/early /2018/08/16/peds.2018-2058.

Index

Acknowledgments

This book would not have been possible without the guidance and support of so many. Thank you to all of my new friends at Callisto Media for the opportunity you have provided and for your confidence in me as a writer and professional.

My gratitude must go to my husband, Clifford, who always understood the importance of my time and creativity with our children and encouraged my sharing and writing about it. Your endless cheerleading (even on the construction sites) means more to me than you could ever know.

I must express appreciation to my parents, Tammy and Raymond Sherman, for their endless support through all my crazy ideas and adventures, even when they don't go quite as planned. Thank you for loving my children so incredibly hard. None of us would be what we are without you.

My appreciation goes, as well, to a few close friends. Katie Switzer, you're a rock star art teacher, toddler mama, and forever friend. Thank you for your help in remembering how toddlers play and how moms of toddlers think. Jon Soderberg, thank you for the "*Go write!*"s, "*Good job, darlin'!*"s, and putting things in perspective when I needed it. Jennifer Tammi Grossi, thanks for the long chats, "Me, too!"s, and endless encouragement that help me keep going in this mom-preneur game.

A special message for my three children, Sawyer, Priscilla, and J.C.: Thank you for bringing your endless inspiration into my life. Your curiosity, wonder, creativity, and laughter sparked each activity in this book and will hopefully go forth to inspire more curiosity, creativity, wonder, and laughter in our world. You are world changers! Parenting you through your *busy toddler years* and every moment since has been the most difficult but the most energizing, most rewarding, and most favorite job I've had in life.

And finally, this would never have happened without the many readers and online supporters of B-InspiredMama.com. Reading messages from you about how you utilize the ideas I share with children and students all around the world helps me see the goodness in our universe and keeps me going. Thank you for making this work I do meaningful far beyond our little family and for filling my heart with joy.

About the Author

KRISSY BONNING-GOULD is a former art teacher with a Master's Degree in K–12 Art Education turned full-time blogging mama. Upon becoming a mom, Krissy founded B-Inspired Mama simply as a creative outlet; however, it ignited a passion within her for blogging and connecting with fellow moms. Over the past 10 years, between pregnancies and playdates for her children, Sawyer, Priscilla, and J.C., Krissy immersed herself in blogging, social media, and content marketing to grow B-InspiredMama.com into an extensive resource of inspiration for kids' crafts, learning fun, kid-friendly recipes, and creative parenting. Follow her fun via email at B-InspiredMama.com/subscribe and on social media by following @BInspiredMama on Twitter and Instagram, and Pinterest.com/BInspiredMama, Facebook.com/BInspiredMama, and Facebook.com/SensoryActivitiesforKids.